GOOD FOOD, GOOD FRIENDS

GOOD FOOD, GOOD FRIENDS

Carol Cooper and Huguette Khan

Penguin Books Canada Ltd., 2801 John Street, Markham, Ontario, Canada L3R 1B4
Penguin Books Ltd., Harmondsworth, Middlesex, England
Penguin Books, 40 West 23rd Street, New York, New York 10010, U.S.A.
Penguin Books Australia Ltd., Ringwood, Victoria, Australia
Penguin Books (N.Z.) Ltd., 182-190 Wairau Road, Auckland 10, New Zealand

Published in 1984

Canadian Cataloguing in Publication Data

Cooper, Carol, 1947-
Good food, good friends

ISBN 0-14-046649-5

1. Dinners and dining. 2. Entertaining. I. Khan, Huguette, 1943- II. Title.
TX737.C6 1984 641.5'4 C84-098572-X

Book design by
Catherine Wilson/Sunkisst Graphics
Photography by
Hal Roth Photography
Food Stylist
Judy Wells
Cover models
Mary Bernard, Glen Taylor, Jennifer Robbins,
Penny & Craig Wells, Gar & Judy Reeves-Stevens
Manufactured in Canada by
Gagne Printing Limited
Typesetting by
Jay Tee Graphics Ltd.

Front cover photography
Clockwise: Crown Roast of Pork (see page 59);
Spinach and Fruit Salad (see page 43);
Antipasto Platter (see page 28); and,
Mazarine Tart (see page 32).

Contents

Acknowledgements

Thanks to our families and friends who taste-tested our recipes and offered helpful suggestions and continued encouragement. Three people who were most generous with their specific talents were Maxine Kelly, Judy Simcoe and Paul Ambrose. An especially warm thank-you goes to our editor, Mary Adachi.

A NOTE ON METRICATION

The recipes in this book are given in both imperial and metric measures. The metric measurements are not exact conversions of the imperial measurements but have been rounded off to standard metric units. The basic proportion of ingredients remains consistent.

Introduction

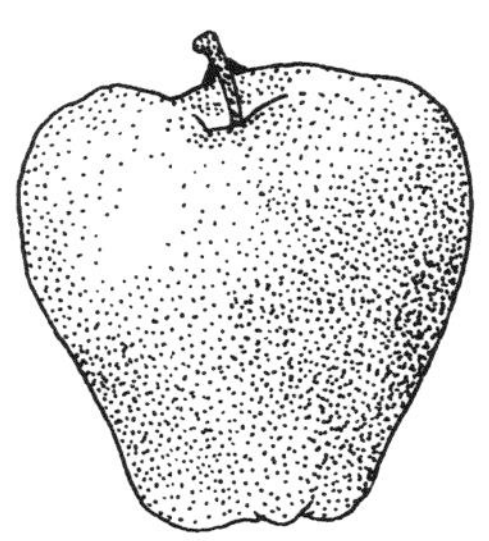

Welcome to a unique, fun and inexpensive way to entertain. The dinner club concept provides a relaxed way to enjoy dinner parties while sharing the work and cost.

Carefully planned menus help to take the guesswork and pressure out of organization and preparation for both experienced and novice cooks. There are recipes to please every palate — from simple, yet interesting fare to exotic, international cuisine.

The basic format is designed to accommodate eight people. They may be four couples or eight individuals. Four people could prepare the food and each invite one guest. It's an ideal and easy way to bring together friends, new neighbours, or residents of an apartment block or neighbourhood. Whether old friends or new, the spirit of co-operation will ensure a relaxed atmosphere and an evening of shared hospitality.

This concept may be expanded and more formalized to include a large number of people. All that's required is a co-ordinator to organize groups of eight, select menus and make the assignments.

Of course, these menus can also be used to prepare a complete dinner party yourself. You can be secure in the knowledge that your meal will be perfectly co-ordinated.

We hope that you and your friends will share many delicious dinners and memorable evenings and experience new dimensions in home entertaining.

Guidelines for a successful dinner club

GENERAL

1 You are the host/hostess only once out of every four dinners.
2 The host/hostess selects the menu and assigns the recipes well in advance, allowing everyone a chance to study the menu, look over the recipes for which he or she is responsible, and anticipate with pleasure the forthcoming event.
3 The host/hostess always prepares the meat dish on the menu. He or she provides the house and the table setting. It can be formal, two small tables or buffet-style. Borrowing and mixing dishes may be necessary and is quite acceptable.
4 Guests prepare their contribution at home and take it, along with a bottle of wine, to the home of the host/hostess.
5 The person who prepares the dish is responsible for all ingredients needed to complete it, such as butter, paprika, toothpicks, etc., adds the finishing touches to the dish and serves it.
6 Please arrive on time! We have allowed one hour between the arrival of guests and starting time of dinner. This interval can be used to enjoy the hors d'oeuvres, start conversations and finish food preparations.

VARIATIONS

1 Have a wine tasting night centered around a menu; for example, German wines only with a German menu. Or try a selection of red wines with a beef dinner or white wines with a seafood dinner.
2 For an international menu provide music, posters, and decorations from that country, display a large map of the area and serve their local wines and beverages.
3 If the group meets regularly, the host/hostess can provide the pre-dinner and after-dinner drinks, since the additional cost will even out over a period of time.

How to use this book

Each menu provides a complete meal, from hors d'oeuvres to dessert, and each recipe serves eight.

Arrival time is set at 8:00 p.m. and dinner at 9:00 p.m., allowing one hour for hors d'oeuvres, conversation and final food preparations.

Follow the co-op chart which divides each menu into four sections that have been carefully calculated to distribute equitably the work and cost. Each couple prepares the assigned dishes at home and takes the food to the home of the host/hostess.

The instructions for preparation are given in two parts — cooking at home and finishing off at the host/hostess'. This two-part method works just as easily if you are planning the entire meal yourself. You can complete the first part well ahead of time and finish the cooking just before dinner; a real boon to the busy host or hostess.

Use the time and temperature chart given at the end of each menu to co-ordinate the time of last minute preparations so that all the dishes are ready at the right time, with a minimum of fuss in the kitchen.

Simple Gourmet Menus

#1	Hors d'oeuvres	Stuffed Cucumber Slices Curried Beef Bites
	Main Course	Pork Tenderloin with Prune and Apple Stuffing Mustard-Glazed Carrots Scalloped Mushrooms Potato Puff
	Dessert	Frozen Raspberry Torte
#2	Hors d'oeuvres	Potted Cheese and Crackers Scotch Eggs
	Main Course	Beef Stroganoff Noodles Carrots and Zucchini Spinach Salad
	Dessert	Lemon-Angel Mold
#3	Hors d'oeuvres	Shrimp Butter and Crackers Bacon Balls
	Main Course	Spiced Lamb Roast Fluffy Potato Casserole Buttery Celery and Corn Green Peas in Sour Cream
	Dessert	Pineapple Dream Flan
#4	Hors d'oeuvres	Antipasto Platter
	First Course	Soup Parisienne
	Main Course	Loin of Pork in Cider Orange-Glazed Parsnips Lima Beans and Green Peas Hearty Peach Salad
	Dessert	Mazarine Tart
#5	Hors d'oeuvres	Salted Nuts Shrimp Toast Canapés
	Main Course	Teriyaki Beef Fried Rice Polynesian-Style Vegetables Oriental Coleslaw
	Dessert	Double Ginger Cloud

#6	Hors d'oeuvres	Water Chestnuts in Barbecue Sauce
		Quiche Tarts
	Main Course	Veal in Ginger Wine
		Zucchini Stuffed with Mushrooms
		Savoury Rice
		Spinach and Fruit Salad
	Dessert	Irish Coffee Mousse
#7	Hors d'oeuvres	Curry Dip with Raw Vegetables
		Teriyaki Meatballs
	Main Course	Halibut or Swordfish Steaks
		Spiced Green Beans
		Crispy Squash Squares
		Spinach-Stuffed Baked Potatoes
	Dessert	Coffee Gateau

Simple Gourmet Menu #1

Hors d'oeuvres	Stuffed Cucumber Slices
	Curried Beef Bites
Main Course	Pork Tenderloin with Fruit Stuffing
	Mustard-Glazed Carrots
	Potato Puff
	Scalloped Mushrooms
Dessert	Frozen Raspberry Torte

Co-op Chart

Host/Hostess	Pork Tenderloin with Fruit Stuffing
Couple A	Curried Beef Bites, Mustard-Glazed Carrots
Couple B	Stuffed Cucumber, Scalloped Mushrooms
Couple C	Potato Puff, Raspberry Torte

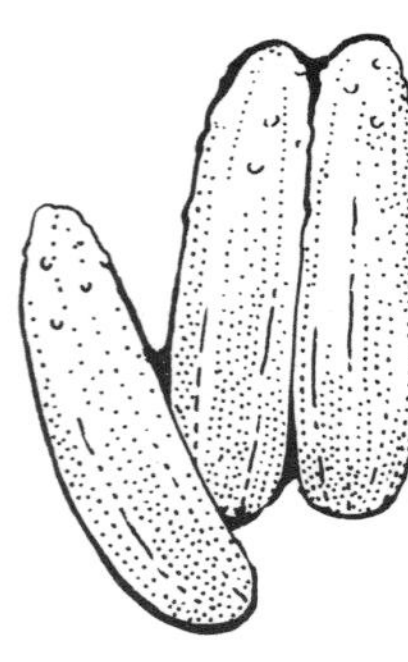

STUFFED CUCUMBER SLICES

Stuffed green olives	1/4 cup (50 mL)
Cream cheese with chives	8 oz (250 g)
Cucumbers	4, each about 5 inches (12 cm) long

1 Chop olives and mix with cream cheese at room temperature. Set aside.

2 Peel or score the cucumbers lengthwise to form alternating green and white strips.

3 Cut both ends off each cucumber and scoop out the seeds. Dry cavity by packing with paper towels.

4 Remove towels and solidly pack each cucumber with one-quarter of the cheese mixture. Wrap in plastic wrap and refrigerate.

Last minute preparation Cut cucumbers into 1/2-inch (1-cm) thick slices and arrange on a plate.

CURRIED BEEF BITES

Filling

Butter	2 Tbsp (25 mL)
Garlic	2 cloves, minced
Fresh ginger	1 slice size of a quarter, minced
Onion	4 tsp (20 mL) minced
Curry powder	1 Tbsp (15 mL)
Ground beef	1/2 lb (250 g)
Tabasco sauce	1 tsp (5 mL)
Salt	1/2 tsp (2 mL)

Pastry

All-purpose flour	2 2/3 cups (650 mL)
Salt	1 tsp (5 mL)
Lard	1/2 cup (125 mL)
Butter	1/3 cup (75 mL)
Cold water	7 to 8 Tbsp (100 to 125 mL)

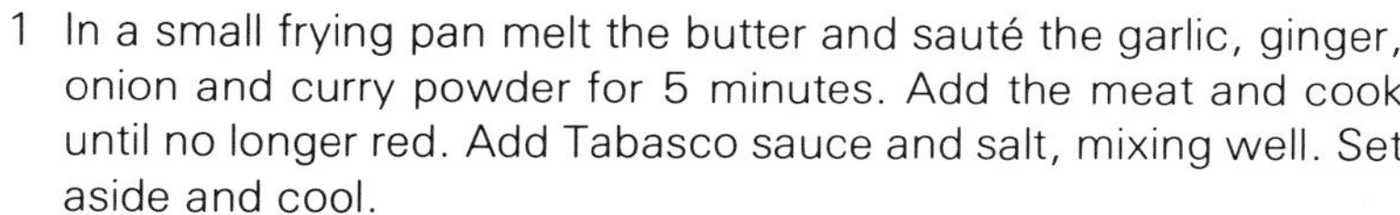

1. In a small frying pan melt the butter and sauté the garlic, ginger, onion and curry powder for 5 minutes. Add the meat and cook until no longer red. Add Tabasco sauce and salt, mixing well. Set aside and cool.
2. Make the pastry by combining flour and salt in a bowl. Cut in lard and butter until they are the size of peas. Add the water a bit at a time, mixing until the flour is moistened and the dough forms a ball.
3. Roll out the pastry and cut into 2-inch (5-cm) circles. Place cool meat mixture on half of the circles, then moisten the edges with water. Cover with remaining circles and press the edges together tightly.
4. Bake at 450°F (230°C) for about 15 minutes or until lightly golden. Remove, cool and store in the refrigerator.

Last minute preparation Reheat the pastries on a cookie sheet at 325°F (160°C) for about 10 minutes or until piping hot.

PORK TENDERLOIN WITH FRUIT STUFFING

Prunes	12 pitted
Tart apples	3
Lemon juice	1 1/2 tsp (7 mL)
Lemon rind	1 tsp (5 mL) finely grated
Fresh bread crumbs	1 cup (250 mL)
Salt	1 tsp (5 mL)
Pepper	1/2 tsp (2 mL)
Pork tenderloin filets	4 large
Oil	2 Tbsp (25 mL)
White wine	2/3 cup (150 mL)
Onion	1/2 cup (125 mL) chopped
Light cream	2/3 cup (150 mL)
Cornstarch	2 Tbsp (25 mL)
Red currant jelly	1 cup (250 mL)

1 In a bowl, cover prunes with warm water and soak for 30 minutes. Drain and chop.

2 Peel and core apples and chop finely. Toss with lemon juice, rind, bread crumbs, salt, pepper and prunes. Set aside.

3 Split the tenderloins lengthwise with a sharp knife, but do not cut all the way through. Press open and flatten slightly.

4 Arrange half of the stuffing on one filet, then top with a second filet and wrap securely with strong thread. Repeat with remaining filets and stuffing.

5 In a large frying pan, heat oil and brown the tenderloins. Transfer to an ovenproof casserole, add wine and onion, cover and bake at 325°F (160°C), allowing 35 minutes per pound (70 minutes per kg).

Last minute preparation Place meat on a warm platter, remove thread and cover. To make gravy, add cream to the casserole and boil gently to reduce the volume to 1 1/4 cups (300 mL). Combine equal amounts of cornstarch and water and add to sauce and cook until smooth. Serve red currant jelly separately.

MUSTARD-GLAZED CARROTS

Carrots	2 lbs (1 kg)
Salt	1 tsp (5 mL)
Butter	3 Tbsp (50 mL)
Prepared mustard	3 Tbsp (50 mL)
Brown sugar	1/4 cup (50 mL)
Fresh parsley	1 Tbsp (15 mL) chopped

1 Clean carrots and slice thinly. Cook in 1 inch (2.5 cm) of water and salt until just barely tender.

2 In a separate saucepan heat butter, mustard, sugar and parsley until syrupy.

3 Drain carrots, reserving 2 Tbsp (25 mL) cooking liquid. Add carrots and liquid to the mustard sauce and mix well. Cover and refrigerate.

Last minute preparation Reheat on the stove top or, covered, in oven at 325°F (160°C) for 15 minutes.

POTATO PUFF

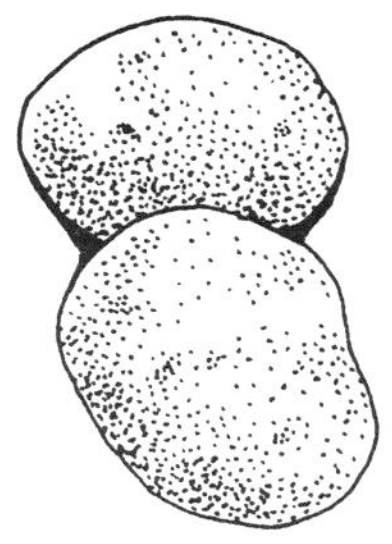

Potatoes	8 medium
Butter	4 Tbsp (65 mL)
Fresh parsley	2 tsp (10 mL) chopped
Salt	1/4 tsp (1 mL)
Cayenne pepper	pinch
Onion	2 tsp (10 mL) minced
Eggs	3

1 Peel, boil and mash potatoes. You will have about 3 cups (750 mL) mashed potatoes. Add butter, parsley, salt, cayenne, and onion.

2 Separate the eggs. Beat the yolks, add to the potatoes and mix well.

3 Beat the egg whites until stiff, then fold them into the potato mixture. Place in a buttered baking dish and dot with remaining butter. Cover and refrigerate.

Last minute preparation Bake, uncovered, at 325°F (160°C) for about 40 minutes, until golden brown.

SCALLOPED MUSHROOMS

Mushrooms	1 1/2 lbs (750 g)
Soft bread crumbs	2 1/2 cups (625 mL)
Butter	2/3 cup (150 mL) melted
Salt	1 tsp (5 mL)
Pepper	1/2 tsp (2 mL)
Leeks	1/3 cup (75 mL) chopped, white part only
Dry white wine or Vermouth	6 Tbsp (100 mL)

1 Clean and slice the mushrooms and layer one-third of the mushrooms on the bottom of a buttered 2-quart (2-L) casserole. Cover with one-third of the bread crumbs and drizzle one-third of the butter over the crumbs. Sprinkle with salt and pepper and chopped leeks.

2 Repeat the layers one more time with the same amounts of mushrooms, crumbs, butter, salt and pepper.

3 Distribute the remaining mushrooms over the top of the casserole and sprinkle with salt and pepper. Pour the wine evenly over the top. Cover and refrigerate.

4 Combine the remaining third of the crumbs and butter and store separately.

Last minute preparation Bake, covered, at 325°F (160°C) for 40 minutes. Uncover, then sprinkle the buttered crumbs over the mushrooms and bake, uncovered, 10 more minutes until the crumbs are toasted. Serve hot.

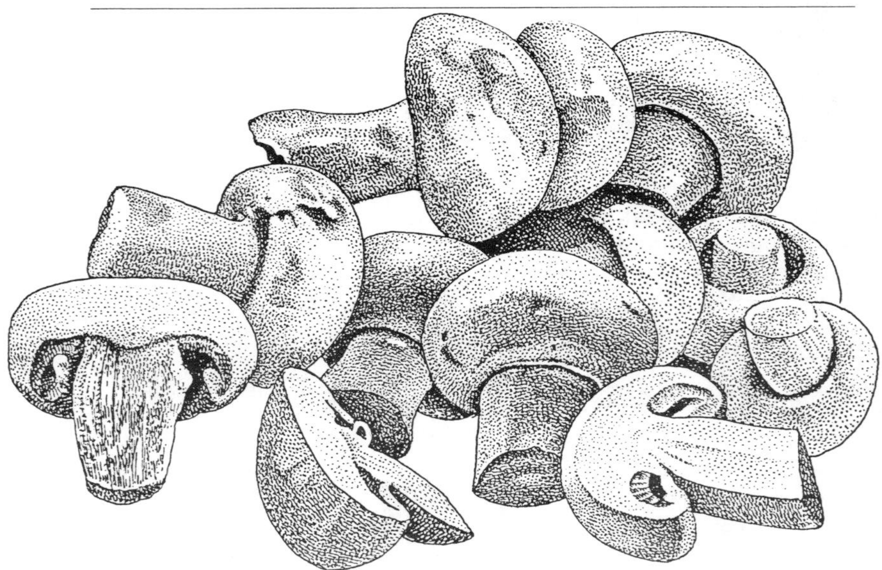

FROZEN RASPBERRY TORTE

Sweetened frozen raspberries	2 10-oz (425-g) packages
Sugar	1 1/4 cups (300 mL)
Water	1/3 cup (75 mL)
Corn syrup	1 tsp (5 mL)
Egg whites	4
Whipping cream	2 cups (500 mL)
Kirsch liqueur	1/4 cup (50 mL)
Icing sugar	1/4 cup (50 mL)
Ladyfingers	16 large
Butter	1/4 cup (50 mL) melted
Fresh raspberries	for garnish, if available

1 Thaw raspberries, purée, then strain to remove the seeds. Discard the seeds. Measure the purée; you should have 2 cups (500 mL).

2 In a small pan combine sugar, water and corn syrup and boil over high heat to the soft ball stage, 238°F (115°C). If you do not have a thermometer, then drop 1 tsp (5 mL) syrup into very cold water and let it stand for one minute. When you touch the syrup it should form into a soft ball that does not hold its shape.

3 With an electric mixer beat egg whites in a large bowl until soft peaks form, then gradually add hot syrup, beating continuously. Continue beating at high speed for 8 minutes, or until meringue cools to room temperature. Fold in raspberry purée.

4 Whip 1 cup (250 mL) cream until stiff, then fold into raspberry-meringue mixture.

5 Whip remaining cream until stiff, then fold in Kirsch and icing sugar.

6 Crush the ladyfingers, combine with melted butter and pat into the bottom of a large spring-form pan. Add half of the raspberry-meringue, then add whipped cream with Kirsch. Spread the remaining raspberry-meringue over the top. Cover and refrigerate at least 6 hours.

Last minute preparation Remove the sides from pan and serve dessert frozen. Garnish with fresh berries if available.

TIME AND TEMPERATURE CHART

6:30	325°F (160°C)	Pork Tenderloin
8:10	325°F (160°C)	Curried Beef Bites
8:20	325°F (160°C)	Scalloped Mushrooms Potato Puff
8:45	325°F (160°C)	Mustard-Glazed Carrots

Simple Gourmet Menu #2

Hors d'oeuvres	Potted Cheese and Crackers
	Scotch Eggs
Main Course	Noodles
	Beef Stroganoff
	Carrots and Zucchini
	Spinach Salad
Dessert	Lemon-Angel Mold

Co-op Chart

Host/Hostess	Beef Stroganoff
Couple A	Scotch Eggs, Noodles
Couple B	Potted Cheese, Carrots and Zucchini
Couple C	Spinach Salad, Lemon-Angel Mold

POTTED CHEESE AND CRACKERS

Cream cheese	8 oz (250 g)
Gruyère or Gouda cheese	2 cups (500 mL) finely shredded
Blue cheese	1/2 cup (125 mL) crumbled
Parmesan cheese	1/4 cup (50 mL) grated
Butter	1/2 cup (125 g)
White wine	2 Tbsp (25 mL)
Garlic powder	1/4 tsp (1 mL)
Pecan pieces	1/2 cup (125 mL) chopped
Crackers	assortment

1 Blend the 4 cheeses, butter, wine and garlic powder together and beat until smooth.

2 Press into a serving dish and sprinkle with pecans. Cover and refrigerate.

Last minute preparation Remove from refrigerator and let stand at room temperature for 20 minutes. Serve with crackers.

SCOTCH EGGS

Eggs	10
Flour	1/4 cup (50 mL)
Dry bread crumbs	1 1/2 cups (375 mL)
Salt	1/2 tsp (2 mL)
Pepper	1/2 tsp (2 mL)
Ground thyme	1/4 tsp (1 mL)
Bulk sausage meat	1 lb (500 g)

1 Hard boil 8 eggs, cool quickly and peel. Pat dry and roll in flour to lightly coat them. Set aside.

2 Combine bread crumbs, salt, pepper and thyme. Beat remaining 2 eggs and set aside.

3 Divide sausage meat into 8 equal portions. With hands moistened in water to prevent sticking, wrap one portion of sausage meat around one cooked egg. Dip wrapped egg into beaten eggs and then into crumbs. Place on baking sheet and repeat with remaining eggs and sausage meat.

4 Bake at 375°F (190°C) for 20 to 25 minutes. Cool, cover and refrigerate.

Last minute preparation Cut eggs into quarters and serve at room temperature.

NOODLES

Salt	1 Tbsp (15 mL)
Egg noodles	12 oz (375 g)
Butter	1/3 cup (75 mL)
Fresh parsley	1 Tbsp (15 mL) chopped

Last minute preparation In a large pot bring 4 quarts (4 L) water to a boil and add salt. Add noodles and cook, uncovered, at a full boil, stirring occasionally, until tender but firm, 5 to 7 minutes. Drain and rinse with cold water, then drain again and rinse with hot water. Toss drained noodles with butter and parsley.

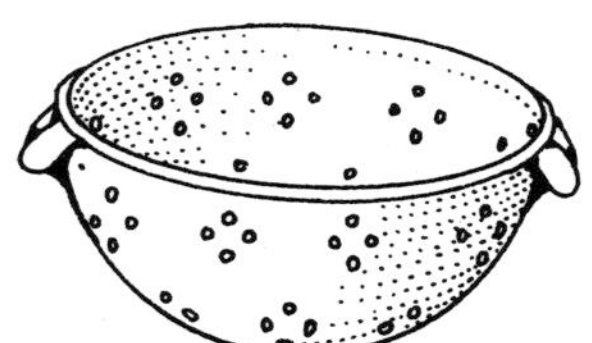

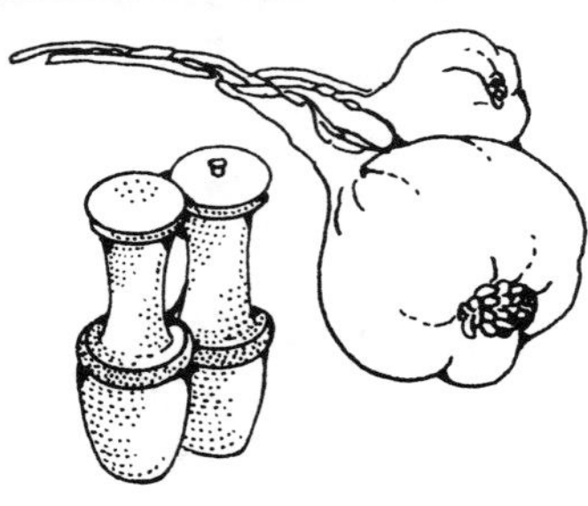

BEEF STROGANOFF

Beef filet, sirloin or porterhouse	2 1/2 lbs (1.2 kg)
Butter	1/2 cup (125 mL)
Onions	2 medium, sliced
Fresh mushrooms	1 lb (500 g), sliced
Garlic	2 cloves, minced
Flour	1/3 cup (75 mL)
Beef stock	1/2 cup (125 mL)
Brandy	1/4 cup (50 mL)
Ketchup	2 Tbsp (25 mL)
Salt	1 1/2 tsp (7 mL)
Pepper	1/2 tsp (2 mL)
Sour cream	1 1/2 cups (375 mL)

1 Cut meat into strips 1/2 inch by 2 inches (1 cm by 5 cm).

2 In a frying pan, melt half the butter, add part of the meat and onions and cook quickly for about 2 minutes. Remove from pan and set aside. Continue with small portions of meat and onions. When completed, cover and refrigerate.

3 Reduce heat and add remaining butter and sauté mushrooms and garlic for 3 minutes. Add flour, and when incorporated, add stock, brandy, ketchup, salt and pepper. Stir until sauce is smooth, then remove from heat. Cover and refrigerate.

Last minute preparation Gently reheat sauce, then add sour cream, meat and onions. Heat through, but do not boil. Serve over hot noodles.

CARROTS AND ZUCCHINI

Zucchini	1 1/2 lbs (750 g)
Carrots	7 medium
Butter	1/4 cup (50 mL)
Water	2 Tbsp (25 mL)
Dried marjoram	1/4 tsp (1 mL)
Salt	1/2 tsp (2 mL)
Pepper	1/4 tsp (1 mL)

1 Wash zucchini, but do not peel. Cut into match-stick size pieces.

2 Peel carrots and also cut them into match-stick size pieces. Store the two vegetables separately.

Last minute preparation At the last minute, melt butter in a large pan and add carrots and water. Cover and bring to a boil. Steam for 2 minutes, then add zucchini, marjoram, salt and pepper. Cook just until zucchini is softened, about 2 to 3 minutes. Put the vegetables in a covered serving dish.

SPINACH SALAD

Fresh spinach	20 oz (560 g)
Bacon	1/2 lb (250 g)
Salt	1 tsp (5 mL)
Pepper	1/4 tsp (1 mL)
Garlic	2 cloves, minced
Dried tarragon	1 tsp (5 mL)
Red wine vinegar	1/3 cup (75 mL)
Olive oil	3/4 cup (175 mL)
Lemon juice	2 tsp (10 mL)
Hard-boiled eggs	2
Red-skinned apple	1 medium

1 Wash spinach and drain. Remove stems and tear the leaves into bite-sized pieces. Wrap in paper towels, place in a plastic bag and refrigerate.

2 Cook bacon until crisp, drain well and crumble, reserving 2 Tbsp (25 mL) bacon drippings.

3 Make the dressing by combining reserved bacon drippings, salt, pepper, garlic, tarragon, vinegar and olive oil. Store in a jar.

4 Chop unpeeled apple into bite-sized pieces and sprinkle with lemon juice. Store in a covered container.

Last minute preparation Peel and chop hard-boiled eggs. Combine spinach, bacon, eggs and apple in a salad bowl. Shake dressing well and add to salad. Toss and serve immediately.

LEMON-ANGEL MOLD

Angel-food cake	1
Eggs	6
Sugar	1 1/2 cups (375 mL)
Fresh lemon juice	3/4 cup (175 mL)
Lemon rind	1 1/2 tsp (7 mL) grated
Unflavoured gelatin	1 envelope
Yellow food colouring	4 drops
Whipping cream	1 cup (250 mL)
Icing sugar	3 Tbsp (50 mL)

1 At least 12 hours before dinner, trim brown crusts from cake and tear the cake into pieces the size of a walnut.

2 Separate the eggs. Beat the yolks, then add 3/4 cup (175 mL) sugar, lemon juice and rind. Cook in the top of a double boiler until the mixture thickens and coats a spoon. Remove from heat.

3 Add gelatin to 1/4 cup (50 mL) cold water. When gelatin has absorbed all the water, stir it into the lemon mixture along with a few drops of yellow food colouring. Cool until partially set.

4 Beat egg whites until almost stiff, then gradually add the remaining 3/4 cup (200 mL) sugar until very stiff. Fold egg whites into partially set lemon mixture.

5 Pour the lemon mixture over the cake pieces, stirring gently to coat. Pack mixture into a large buttered bundt pan or attractive mold. A pretty glass bowl can also be used, but it should not be buttered. Chill until firm, at least 10 to 12 hours.

6 Remove the cake by inverting the mold or bundt pan over a serving plate.

7 Whip the cream and icing sugar and frost the mold. If dessert is in a glass bowl, top with the whipped cream. Store in the refrigerator. Note: Do not whip cream or frost mold too far in advance.

Last minute preparation Serve this dessert well chilled.

TIME AND TEMPERATURE CHART

8:40	Stove Top	Noodles
8:45	Stove Top	Beef Stroganoff
8:50	Stove Top	Carrots and Zucchini

Simple Gourmet Menu #3

Hors d'oeuvres	Shrimp Butter and Crackers
	Bacon Balls
Main Course	Spiced Lamb Roast
	Fluffy Potato Casserole
	Buttery Celery and Corn
	Green Peas in Sour Cream
Dessert	Pineapple Dream Flan

Co-op Chart

Host/Hostess	Spiced Lamb Roast
Couple A	Buttery Celery and Corn, Pineapple Dream Flan
Couple B	Shrimp Butter, Green Peas
Couple C	Bacon Balls, Potato Casserole

SHRIMP BUTTER AND CRACKERS

Baby or broken shrimp	4 oz (113 g)
Lemon juice	1 tsp (5 mL)
Green onion	1, finely chopped
Cream cheese	8 oz (250 g), softened
Butter	3 Tbsp (50 mL), softened
Mayonnaise	3 Tbsp (50 mL)
Horseradish	1 Tbsp (15 mL)
Crackers	assortment

1 Clean shrimp and remove any pieces of shell. Set aside one large shrimp for garnish. Add lemon juice and onion to remaining shrimps and mash with a fork.

2 Whip the cream cheese, butter, mayonnaise and horseradish together until fluffy. Add shrimp mixture and beat again.

3 Put in a bowl and garnish with whole shrimp. Cover and refrigerate.

Last minute preparation Remove from refrigerator 30 minutes before serving and serve with crackers.

BACON BALLS

Stuffed olives	1 13.2-oz (375-mL) jar
Bacon	1/2 lb (250 g)

1 Cut bacon strips into quarters or thirds. Wrap around an olive and secure with a toothpick.

2 Place on a cookie sheet, cover and refrigerate.

Last minute preparation Broil until bacon is done, turning once or twice. Serve warm.

SPICED LAMB ROAST

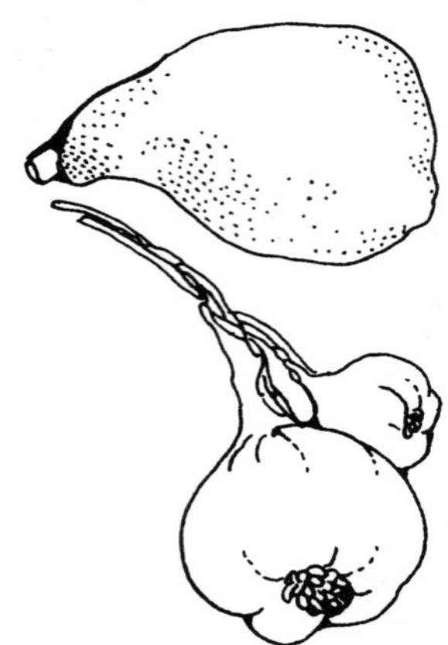

Olive oil	1/4 cup (50 mL)
Boned leg of lamb	4 to 5 lbs (2.5 kg)
Onions	3
Garlic	3 cloves, minced
Whole cloves	10
Tomatoes	3, peeled and chopped
Salt	1 tsp (5 mL)
Cinnamon stick	2 inches (5 cm)
Lemon peel	1 tsp (5 mL) grated
Tomato juice	1 cup (250 mL)
Water	1 1/2 cups (375 mL)
Sherry	1/2 cup (125 mL)
Cornstarch	2 Tbsp (25 mL)

Note This recipe is best cooked ahead, chilled and reheated when needed.

1 In a Dutch oven heat oil over medium high heat, add meat and brown well on all sides, then remove.

2 Chop 2 onions and add to pan with garlic. Cook, stirring, for 3 minutes. Stick cloves into remaining onion and add with tomatoes, salt, cinnamon stick and lemon peel to pan.

3 Return roast to pan, add tomato juice, water and sherry and bring to a boil. Reduce heat, cover and simmer until very tender, about 2 to 3 hours.

4 Uncover to cool, then refrigerate, covered.

Last minute preparation Remove solidified fat from the liquid in the pan, cover and heat for 30 minutes. Reduce heat and simmer for an additional 20 minutes. Remove meat and keep warm in oven. Mix 1/4 cup (50 mL) water with cornstarch until smooth, then add to pan juices. Stir and cook until thickened and smooth. Slice the meat and serve the gravy separately.

FLUFFY POTATO CASSEROLE

Potatoes	6 large, peeled
Cream cheese	4 oz (125 g)
Sour cream	3/4 cup (175 mL)
Onion salt	1 1/2 tsp (7 mL)
Salt	1/2 tsp (2 mL)
Pepper	1/2 tsp (2 mL)
French fried onion rings	1 3 1/2-oz (85-g) can, optional

1 Cook potatoes in boiling salted water, drain and mash until smooth.

2 Add cream cheese, sour cream, onion salt, salt and pepper. Beat with electric mixer until smooth and fluffy.

3 Spoon into a greased 2-quart (2-L) baking dish. Cover and refrigerate.

Last minute preparation Sprinkle fried onions over top and bake, uncovered, at 300°F (150°C) for about 35 minutes.

BUTTERY CELERY AND CORN

Black olives	10
Butter	1/3 cup (75 mL)
Celery	3 cups (750 mL) finely sliced
Frozen corn kernels	2 cups (500 mL)
Salt	1 tsp (5 mL)

1 Pit olives and cut into rings.

Last minute preparation In a medium-sized saucepan melt butter. Add celery and sauté for 5 minutes, then add corn. Cover and cook for 10 more minutes. Add olives and salt and mix well.

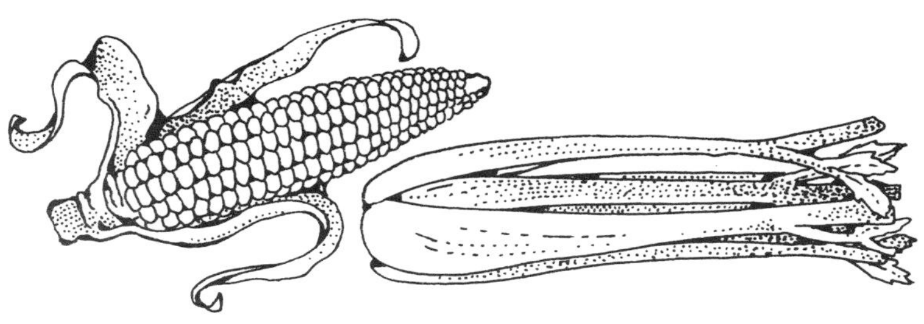

GREEN PEAS IN SOUR CREAM

Sour cream	1 cup (250 mL)
Horseradish	1 tsp (5 mL)
Salt	1/2 tsp (2 mL)
Pepper	1/4 tsp (1 mL)
Lemon juice	4 tsp (20 mL)
Worcestershire sauce	1/2 tsp (2 mL)
Sugar	1 tsp (5 mL)
Lettuce leaves	6 large
Green onions	4
Frozen small green peas	20 oz (700 g)
Tart red apples	2

1 To make the dressing, combine sour cream, horseradish, salt, pepper, lemon juice, Worcestershire sauce and sugar. Store, covered, in refrigerator.

2 Wash lettuce leaves, wrap in paper towels and store in plastic bag in refrigerator.

3 Slice green onions and store separately.

Last minute preparation Put frozen peas into a colander and run hot tap water over them until they are just thawed. Core but do not peel the apples and chop. Combine apple with peas, onion and dressing. Line salad bowl with lettuce leaves and pile salad mixture in the centre.

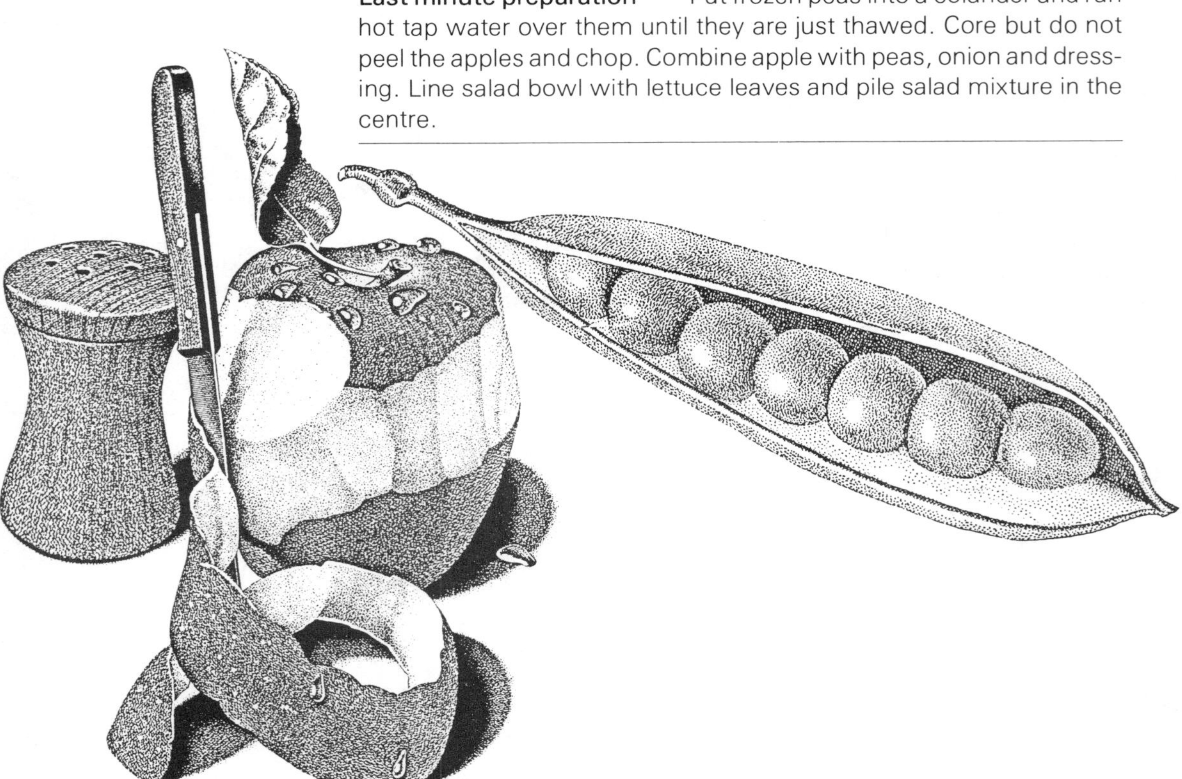

PINEAPPLE DREAM FLAN

All-purpose flour	1 1/2 cups (375 mL)
Butter	1 1/2 cups (375 mL), softened
Egg	1 large, well-beaten
Icing sugar	2 1/2 cups (625 mL)
Unsweetened crushed pineapple	1 14-oz (398-mL) can
Whipping cream	1 1/2 cups (375 mL)

1 Mix flour and 3/4 cup (175 mL) butter together and pat into bottom of a 9-inch (3-L) spring-form pan. Bake at 325°F (160°C) for 12 minutes until golden. Cool to room temperature.

2 Beat remaining 3/4 cup (175 mL) butter, egg and icing sugar together until smooth and creamy, then spread over the cooled crust.

3 Drain crushed pineapple in a sieve for 10 minutes and squeeze to extract all the juices. Whip cream until stiff, then fold in 2 Tbsp (25 mL) icing sugar and drained pineapple. Spread over flan and store in refrigerator.

Last minute preparation Serve cold and cut into small pieces as it is very rich.

TIME AND TEMPERATURE CHART

8:00	Broil	Bacon Balls
8:00	Stove top	Spiced Lamb Roast
8:25	300°F (150°C)	Potato Casserole
8:45	Stove top	Buttery Celery and Corn

Simple Gourmet Menu #4

Hors d'oeuvres	Antipasto Platter
First Course	Soup Parisienne
Main Course	Loin of Pork in Cider
	Orange-Glazed Parsnips
	Lima Beans and Green Peas
	Hearty Peach Salad
Dessert	Mazarine Tart

Co-op Chart

Host/Hostess	Loin of Pork in Cider
Couple A	Antipasto Platter, Peach Salad
Couple B	Soup Parisienne, Glazed Parsnips
Couple C	Lima Beans and Peas, Mazarine Tart

ANTIPASTO PLATTER

Salami	1/2 lb (250 g), assorted
Cheese	3/4 lb (375 g), assorted
Solid packed tuna	1 7.7-oz (220-g) can
Green olives	30, approximately
Black olives	30, approximately
Marinated artichoke hearts	2 6-oz (170-mL) jars
Pickled pimento	1 small jar
Marinated mushrooms	1 4-oz (125-mL) jar
Tomatoes	3
Hard-boiled eggs	3

1 Roll salami into tubes. Cut cheese into chunks or slices. Cover and refrigerate.

Last minute preparation Drain tuna, olives, artichokes, pimento and mushrooms. Cut tomatoes and eggs into wedges. On a large platter put the tuna in the centre and arrange remaining ingredients in an attractive pattern. Provide small plates when serving.

SOUP PARISIENNE

Leeks	2
Onions	2 medium
Bacon	6 strips
Potatoes	4 medium
Butter	4 tsp (20 mL)
Bay leaves	2
Ground thyme	1/2 tsp (2 mL)
Pepper	1/2 tsp (2 mL)
Chicken stock	8 cups (2 L)
Whipping cream	2/3 cup (150 mL)
Fresh parsley	2 tsp (10 mL) chopped

1 Wash leeks thoroughly and slice white and light green parts finely. Dice the onions and bacon. Peel potatoes and cut into 1/4-inch (5-mm) cubes.

2 In a large saucepan, heat 2 tsp (10 mL) butter. Add bacon and fry for 5 minutes. Add onions, leeks, bay leaves, thyme and pepper and fry for another 5 minutes. Add diced potatoes and sauté lightly for 2 more minutes.

3 Add stock and stir well. Cover and simmer for 1 hour. Cool and refrigerate.

Last minute preparation Reheat soup until very hot, then add cream, remaining 2 tsp (10 mL) butter and parsley. Stir to combine, but do not boil. Serve in preheated bowls.

LOIN OF PORK IN CIDER

Pork loin roast	10 ribs
Salt	1 Tbsp (15 mL)
Pepper	1 tsp (5 mL)
Baking apples	8
Carrots	3, peeled and quartered
Onions	8 large
Apple cider	1 1/2 cups (375 mL)
Dried rosemary	1 tsp (5 mL)
Flour	2 Tbsp (25 mL)
Cognac	1/4 cup (50 mL)

1 Sprinkle pork with salt and pepper and roast at 375°F (190°C) for 1 1/2 hours.

2 Core the apples and peel the onions but leave them whole.

3 Pour off the fat in the roast pan. Arrange apples, carrots and onions around the roast, add 1 cup (250 mL) cider and rosemary and bake for 1 1/4 hours longer at 325°F (160°C). Baste the roast, apples, carrots and onions frequently.

Last minute preparation To serve, slice meat and place with the apples, carrots and onions on a platter. Combine flour and 2 Tbsp (25 mL) water. Skim fat from gravy and over low heat stir in flour mixture until thickened. Add Cognac and remaining 1/2 cup (125 mL) cider, stirring constantly until heated. Pour some sauce over the meat and serve the remainder separately.

ORANGE-GLAZED PARSNIPS

Parnsips	3 lbs (1.5 kg)
Butter	1/4 cup (50 mL)
Orange marmalade	1/2 cup (125 mL)
Ground ginger	1/4 tsp (1 mL)
Water	1/3 cup (75 mL)
Seedless orange	1 large, peeled

1 Peel parsnips and cut into julienne pieces. Cook in boiling salted water until just tender, then drain well.

2 In a small pot combine butter, marmalade, ginger and water and boil for 5 minutes. Add drained parsnips and stir to glaze well. Place in ovenproof serving dish, cover and refrigerate.

3 Cut orange in half and slice to form half circles. Store separately.

Last minute preparation Spoon glaze from bottom of dish to cover parsnips. Heat at 325°F (160°C) for 15 minutes, watching that it does not burn. Garnish with orange slices just before serving.

LIMA BEANS AND GREEN PEAS

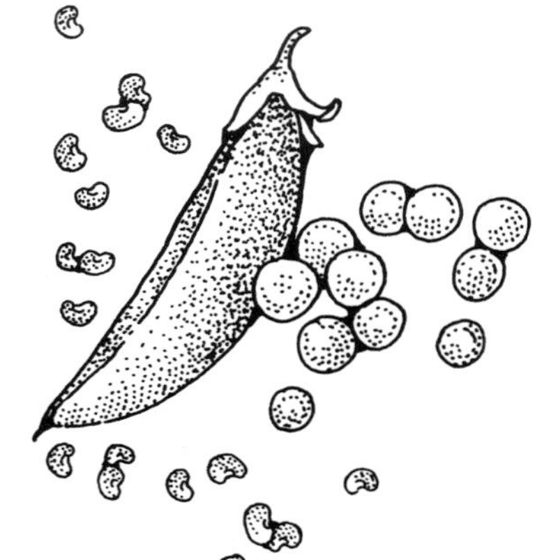

Fresh or frozen lima beans	20 oz (700 g)
Fresh or frozen small green peas	20 oz (700 g)
Green onions	3, chopped
Dried basil	1 1/2 tsp (7 mL)
Salt	1 1/2 tsp (7 mL)
Butter	1/3 cup (75 mL)
Water	1/3 cup (75 mL)

1 In a buttered 2-quart (2-L) casserole combine all ingredients. Cover and refrigerate.

Last minute preparation Bake, covered, at 325°F (160°C) for 45 minutes, or until vegetables are just tender, stirring occasionally. Serve hot.

HEARTY PEACH SALAD

Sweet red peppers	1 lb (500 g)
Smoked ham	1/4 lb (125 g)
Tomatoes	4 large
Dry mustard	1 Tbsp (15 mL)
Sugar	1 Tbsp (15 mL)
Salt	1 tsp (5 mL)
Wine vinegar	1/3 cup (75 mL)
Olive oil	1/3 cup (75 mL)
Water	1/3 cup (75 mL)
Fresh peaches	1/2 lb (250 g) or 3 medium
Lettuce leaves	8

1 Wash and seed peppers and cut into strips. Cut ham into thin strips. Cube tomatoes. Store in separate containers.

2 Make dressing by thoroughly combining mustard, sugar, salt, vinegar, olive oil and water. Store in a jar.

Last minute preparation Skin peaches, remove stones and slice; combine with peppers, ham and tomatoes. Pour dressing over salad and let stand until serving time, about 1/2 hour. Serve in a bowl lined with lettuce leaves.

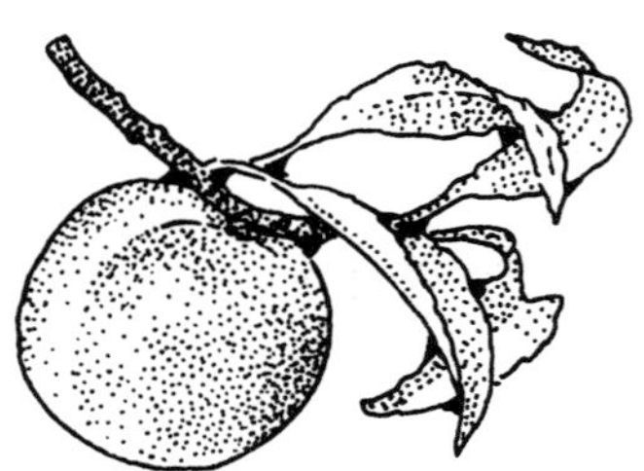

MAZARINE TART

Pastry	for 9-inch (3-L) pan
Raspberry jam	2/3 cup (150 mL)
Butter	2/3 cup (150 mL), softened
Sugar	1 cup (250 mL)
Ground almonds	1 cup (250 mL)
Almond extract	1/2 tsp (2 mL)
Eggs	2
Flour	1/3 cup (75 mL)
Icing sugar	1/2 cup (125 mL)
Lemon juice	2 tsp (10 mL)

1 Roll out pastry to fit bottom and 1 inch (2.5 cm) up the side of a 9-inch (3-L) spring-form pan. Spread 1/3 cup (75 mL) jam on the dough and chill.

2 Combine butter and sugar and add ground almonds, extract and eggs, one at a time, beating well after each addition. Stir in flour and combine well. Spoon over jam layer in pan and bake at 350°F (180°C) for 35 minutes.

3 Cool, release side from pan and place on a serving plate. The cake can be frozen at this stage and defrosted 2 hours before proceeding.

4 No more than 24 hours before serving, spread the remaining 1/3 cup (75 mL) jam on top of cake. Mix icing sugar and lemon juice and drizzle over jam. Cover carefully and refrigerate.

Last minute preparation Cut and let sit at room temperature for 30 minutes before serving.

TIME AND TEMPERATURE CHART

6:00	375°F (190°C)	Loin of Pork in Cider
7:45	325°F (160°C)	Lower oven temperature, leave roast in
8:25	325°F (160°C)	Lima Beans and Peas
8:50	Stove top	Soup Parisienne
8:55	325°F (160°C)	Glazed Parsnips

Clockwise: Potted Cheese, on bread board (page 18); Spinach Salad (page 21); Carrots and Zucchini (page 20); Beef Stroganoff (page 20).

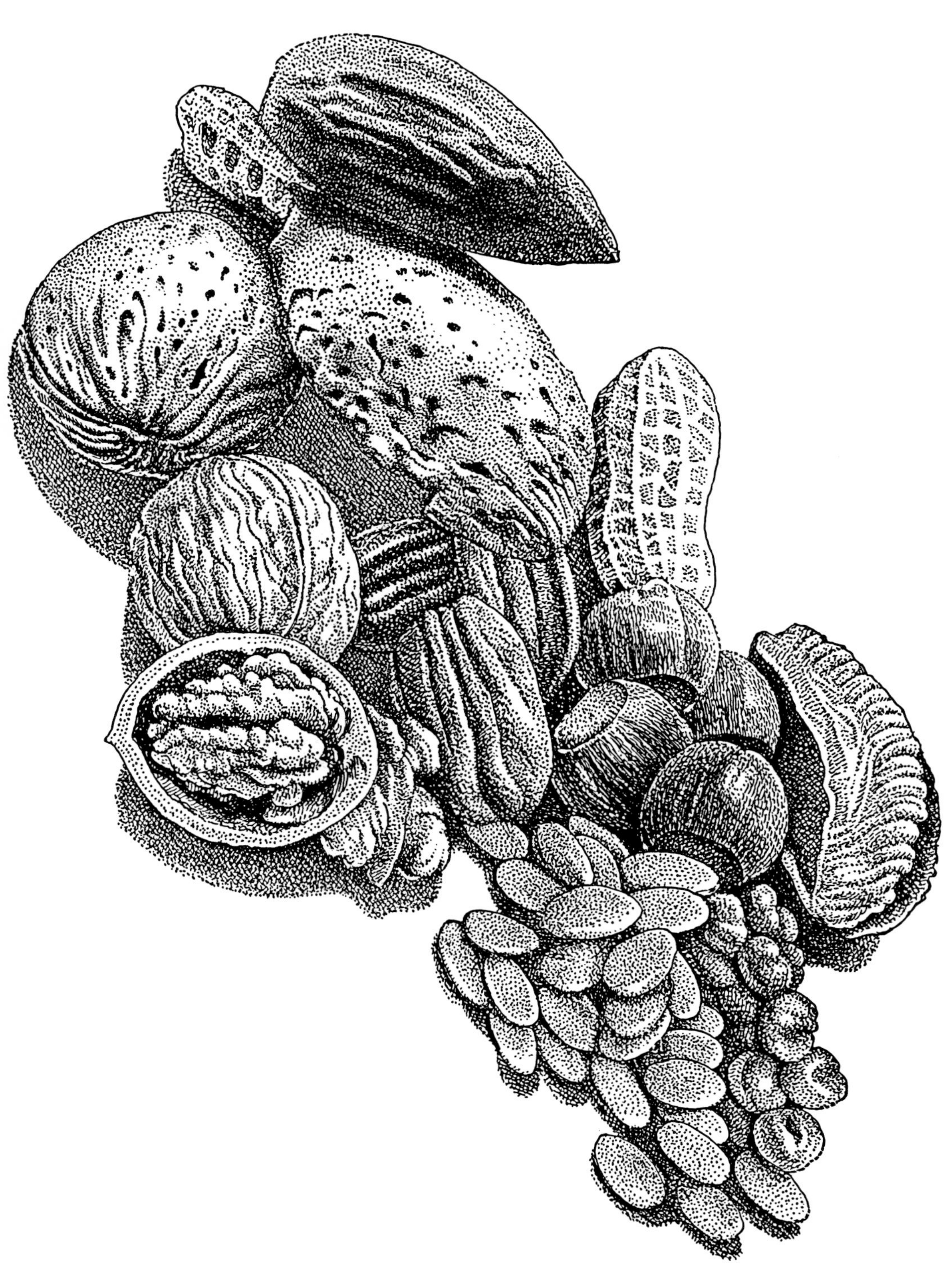

Simple Gourmet Menu #5

Hors d'oeuvres	Salted Nuts
	Shrimp Toast Canapés
Main Course	Teriyaki Beef
	Fried Rice
	Polynesian-Style Vegetables
	Oriental Coleslaw
Dessert	Double Ginger Cloud

Co-op Chart

Host/Hostess	Teriyaki Beef
Couple A	Salted Nuts, Polynesian Vegetables
Couple B	Shrimp Toast, Oriental Coleslaw
Couple C	Fried Rice, Double Ginger Cloud

SALTED NUTS

Egg white	1
Tabasco sauce	1/4 tsp (1 mL)
Whole almonds	1 cup (250 mL)
Whole filberts (hazelnuts)	1 cup (250 mL)
Sea salt	4 tsp (20 mL)
Garlic salt	1/2 tsp (2 mL)

1 Beat egg white and Tabasco in medium-sized bowl until frothy. Add nuts and toss to moisten.

2 Put sea salt and garlic salt in a plastic bag, add the moist nuts and shake. Arrange nuts in a single layer on a lightly greased baking pan. Bake at 300°F (150°C) until golden, about 20 minutes. Cool and store in an airtight container.

Last minute preparation You won't have to pass these more than once; nut-lovers will help themselves!

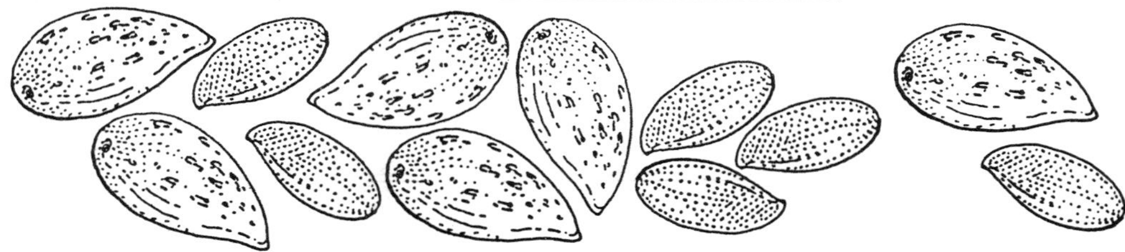

SHRIMP TOAST CANAPÉS

Shelled raw shrimp	1/2 lb (250 g)
Green onions	2
Water chestnuts	5
Garlic salt	1/4 tsp (1 mL)
Pepper	1/8 tsp (0.5 mL)
Lemon juice	1 1/2 tsp (7 mL)
Sugar	1/4 tsp (1 mL)
Egg white	1
Sandwich bread	8 thin slices
Butter	2 Tbsp (25 mL) melted

1 Clean shrimp. Chop shrimp, onions and water chestnuts together very finely or use a food processor.

2 Add garlic salt, pepper, lemon juice, sugar and unbeaten egg white and mix until well blended. Cover and refrigerate.

3 Trim crusts from bread and toast one side under the broiler. Remove from oven, cool and turn over. Cover and set aside.

Last minute preparation Spread shrimp mixture on untoasted side of bread, then brush with melted butter. Broil until shrimp mixture turns pink. Remove from oven, cut into quarters and serve hot.

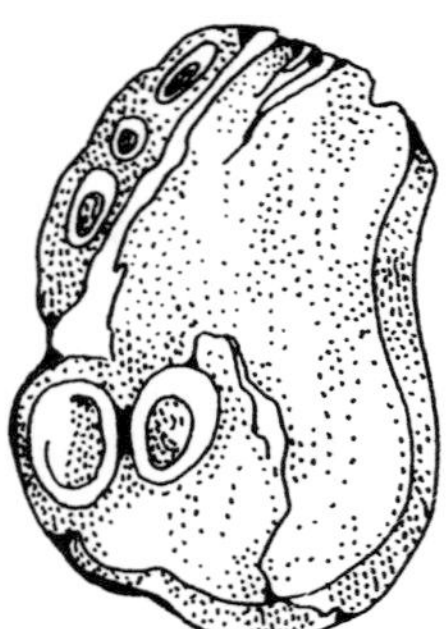

TERIYAKI BEEF

Garlic	2 large cloves, minced
Fresh ginger	1 tsp (5 mL) minced
Green onions	2, finely chopped
Soy sauce	1 cup (250 mL)
Sugar	1/3 cup (75 mL)
Dry sherry	1/3 cup (75 mL)
Sirloin steak	4 lbs (2 kg), 1 inch (2.5 cm) thick

1 Combine garlic, ginger, green onions, soy sauce, sugar and sherry. Pour over meat and marinate in refrigerator for 4 hours, turning the meat at least once an hour.

Last minute preparation Broil or barbecue the steak 5 minutes each side, or as desired. Meanwhile heat the marinade until warm. Slice the meat diagonally across the grain for very tender meat. Place strips on a platter and drizzle some warm marinade over the top. Serve the rest separately.

FRIED RICE

Long grain rice	1 2/3 cups (400 mL)
Water	3 1/3 cups (825 mL)
Salt	1 1/2 tsp (7 mL)
Oil	3/4 cup (175 mL)
Cooked ham	1/3 cup (75 mL) chopped
Soy sauce	1/3 cup (75 mL)
Eggs	5, lightly beaten
Green onions	2/3 cup (150 mL) finely chopped
Frozen or fresh green peas	1/3 cup (75 mL), cooked

1 Rinse rice under cold water until water runs clear. In a medium-sized pot bring water to a boil and add salt and rice. Return to the boil, then reduce heat and simmer, covered, for 15 minutes. Fluff with a fork. If any water remains, cover and let sit for 10 minutes.

2 Spread cooked rice and in a flat roasting pan and heat 20 to 30 minutes at 250°F (130°C) until dry, stirring occasionally. Remove from oven and cool. Rice can be prepared well in advance, even one day ahead.

3 Heat oil in a large skillet. Add ham and fry until lightly browned. Add rice and soy sauce and continue cooking for 5 minutes.

4 Add lightly beaten eggs and cook and stir until rice is well coated. Add onions and green peas and put in an ovenproof serving dish and store in refrigerator.

Last minute preparation: Heat at 350°F (180°C) for 20 minutes. Remove just before broiling the meat, and keep covered.

POLYNESIAN-STYLE VEGETABLES

Fresh vegetables — broccoli, carrots, cauliflower, celery, green or yellow beans, snow peas	3 cups (750 mL), assortment
Green or red pepper	1 large
Unsweetened pineapple chunks	1 14-oz (398-mL) can
Onion	1 cup (250 mL) chopped
Butter	3 Tbsp (50 mL)
Soy sauce	3 Tbsp (50 mL)
Fresh ginger	2 tsp (10 mL) minced
Cornstarch	4 tsp (20 mL)
Water	1/3 cup (75 mL)
Water chestnuts	1 10-oz (284-mL) can, sliced

1 Cut vegetables into bite-sized pieces. Cut pepper into 1-inch (2.5-cm) squares. Drain pineapple and reserve juice.

2 In saucepan sauté onion in butter until tender but not brown. Add pineapple juice, vegetables, pepper, soy sauce and ginger. Bring to a boil, then reduce heat, cover and simmer for 5 minutes, or until vegetables are almost tender.

3 Remove vegetables with a slotted spoon and plunge into ice-cold water. Drain, then place in an ovenproof serving dish.

4 Blend cornstarch and water and add to sauce in saucepan. Cook and stir until sauce is thick and bubbly. Cool.

5 Add cooled sauce, pineapple chunks and water chestnuts to vegetables and mix gently. Cover and refrigerate.

Last minute preparation Heat, covered, at 350°F (180°C) until heated through, approximately 15 to 20 minutes. Do not overcook.

ORIENTAL COLESLAW

Green cabbage or bok choy	3 cups (750 mL) shredded
Green onions	2, chopped
Bean sprouts	2 cups (500 mL)
Sugar	2 Tbsp (25 mL)
White wine or rice vinegar	1/4 cup (50 mL)
Sesame or peanut oil	2 Tbsp (25 mL)
Garlic	1 clove, minced
Salt	1/ tsp (2 mL)

1 Combine cabbage, green onions and bean sprouts in a bowl.

2 Make dressing by combining sugar, vinegar, oil, garlic and salt. Pour over vegetables and toss well. Cover and refrigerate at least one hour.

Last minute preparation Serve chilled.

DOUBLE GINGER CLOUD

Fresh ginger	2 tsp (10 mL) grated
Brandy	3/4 cup (175 mL)
Whipping cream	3 cups (750 mL)
Icing sugar	1/2 cup (125 mL)
Angostura bitters	2 dashes
Ginger cookies (preferably Pantry brand)	1 12-oz (350-g) package, crushed

1 Soak ginger in brandy for 2 hours.

2 Whip cream until thick, adding the sugar 2 Tbsp (25 mL) at a time. When stiff fold in brandy mixture and Angostura bitters.

3 Layer cream and crumbs alternately in parfait glasses, finishing with a layer of cream. Refrigerate at least 6 hours.

Last minute preparation Serve this dessert cold.

TIME AND TEMPERATURE CHART

8:00	Broil	Shrimp Toast
8:30	350°F (180°C)	Fried Rice
8:50		Remove all dishes from over
8:50	Broil	Teriyaki Beef

Simple Gourmet Menu #6

Hors d'oeuvres	Water Chestnuts in Barbecue Sauce Quiche Tarts
Main Course	Veal in Ginger Wine Zucchini Stuffed with Mushrooms Savoury Rice Spinach and Fruit Salad
Dessert	Irish Coffee Mousse

Co-op Chart

Host/Hostess	Veal in Ginger Wine
Couple A	Water Chestnuts, Stuffed Zucchini
Couple B	Quiche Tarts, Savoury Rice
Couple C	Spinach and Fruit Salad, Irish Coffee Mousse

WATER CHESTNUTS IN BARBECUE SAUCE

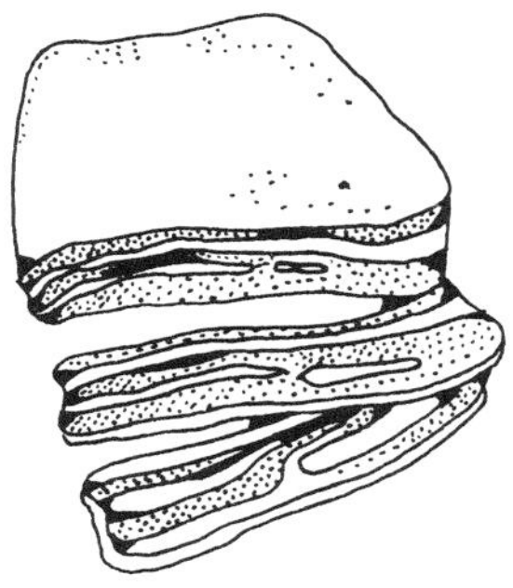

Bacon	1 lb (500 g)
Water chestnuts	2 10-oz (284-mL) cans
Chili sauce	1/2 cup (125 mL)
Catalina French dressing	1/ cup (125 mL)
Brown sugar	1/ cup (125 mL)

1 Cut bacon strips into two or three pieces. Wrap one piece aroud a water chestnut and secure with a toothpick. Place in a single layer in a medium-sized baking dish.

2 Combine chili sauce, dressing and brown sugar and pour over bacon-wrapped water chestnuts. Bake at 350 °F (180 °C) for 45 minutes, turning once. Cool, cover and refrigerate.

Last minute preparation Reheat, uncovered, at 350 °F (180 °F) until hot and bubbling, about 10 minutes.

QUICHE TARTS

Pastry

All-purpose flour	1 1/3 cups (325 mL) sifted
Salt	1/2 tsp (2 mL)
Shortening	1/2 cup (125 mL)
Cold water	3 to 4 Tbsp (50 to 65 mL)

Filling

Bacon	12 slices
Onion	1/3 cup (75 mL) finely chopped
Swiss cheese	1 cup (250 mL) shredded
Eggs	4
Light cream	2 cups (500 mL)
Salt	3/4 tsp (3 mL)
Nutmeg	1/4 tsp (1 mL)
Cayenne pepper	pinch

1 To make pastry, combine flour and 1/2 tsp (2 mL) salt, then cut in shortening until it is the size of peas. Slowly add cold water, mixing until the dough clings together. Chill for one hour.

2 Roll out pastry and line 24 small tart tins.

3 Fry bacon until crisp, then crumble. Mix bacon, onion and shredded cheese and distribute evenly into tart shells.

4 Beat eggs, then add cream, salt, nutmeg and cayenne. Pour mixture into pastry shells. Bake at 375°F (190°C) for 15 minutes. Cool and refrigerate.

Last minute preparation Serve at room temperature or warmed in 350°F (180°C) oven for 5 to 10 minutes.

VEAL IN GINGER WINE

Veal 2 1/2 lbs (1 kg), cut into 10 slices, 1/2 inch (1 cm) thick
Flour 3/4 cup (175 mL)
Salt 1 1/2 tsp (7 mL)
Pepper 1 tsp (5 mL)
Paprika 4 tsp (20 mL)
Butter 1/2 cup (125 mL)
Olive oil 1 Tbsp (15 mL)
Chicken stock 1/2 cup (125 mL)
Ginger wine 3/4 cup (175 mL)
Lemon juice 1 Tbsp (15 mL)
Lemon rind 1 tsp (5 mL) grated
Sour cream 1/2 cup (125 mL)
Instant coffee granules 1/4 tsp (1 mL)
Lemons 2, sliced

1 Trim any fat from veal and pound to 1/4-inch (5-mm) thickness.

2 Combine flour, 1 tsp (5 mL) salt, 1/2 tsp (2 mL) pepper and 1/2 tsp (2 mL) paprika.

3 In a large heavy frying pan heat butter and oil over moderate heat. Dredge veal in seasoned flour and sauté until golden brown, approximately 1 minute on each side. Remove veal to platter and store in refrigerator.

4 Add stock to the frying pan and bring it to a boil, stirring constantly while deglazing pan. Reduce heat, add wine and simmer for 5 minutes.

5 Add lemon juice, grated rind, sour cream, 1/2 tsp (2 mL) salt, 1/2 tsp (2 mL) pepper and coffee granules and simmer for 2 to 3 minutes. Remove from heat and set aside.

Last minute preparation Fifteen minutes before serving, gently reheat sauce and add veal. Continue to heat until veal is very warm, watching that sauce does not burn. Arrange veal on a serving platter and top each piece with a lemon slice and sprinkle remaining paprika.

ZUCCHINI STUFFED WITH MUSHROOMS

Zucchini	4 medium
Oil	2 Tbsp (25 mL)
Butter	3 Tbsp (50 mL)
Fresh mushrooms	1 cup (250 mL) chopped
Garlic	1 large clove, minced
Onion	3 Tbsp (50 mL) finely chopped
Dry sherry	2 Tbsp (25 mL)
Cooked ham	2/3 cup (150 mL) chopped
Salt	1/4 tsp (1 mL)
Pepper	1/2 tsp (2 mL)
Sour cream	3 Tbsp (50 mL)
Dry bread crumbs	3 Tbsp (50 mL)
Fresh parsley	1 1/2 tsp (7 mL) finely chopped

1 Cut zucchini in half lengthwise and brush with oil. Broil for 4 to 5 minutes until soft.

2 Scoop out centre and finely chop flesh.

3 In a large frying pan melt butter and sauté chopped zucchini, mushrooms, garlic and onion for 5 minutes. Add sherry, ham, salt, pepper and sour cream and stir well. Remove from heat.

4 Stuff zucchini shells with mushroom mixture and place in a buttered baking dish. Sprinkle tops with bread crumbs and chopped parsley. Cover and refrigerate.

Last minute preparation Bake at 350°F (180°C) for 25 minutes, or until bubbling. Serve piping hot.

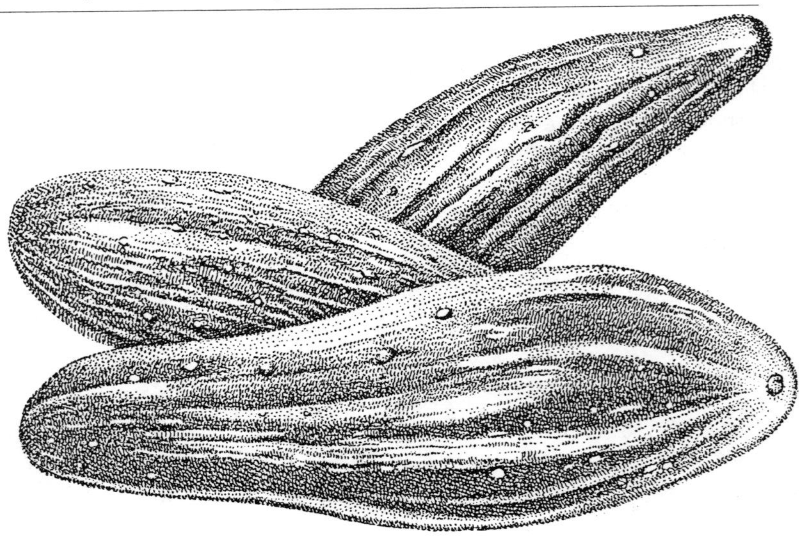

SAVOURY RICE

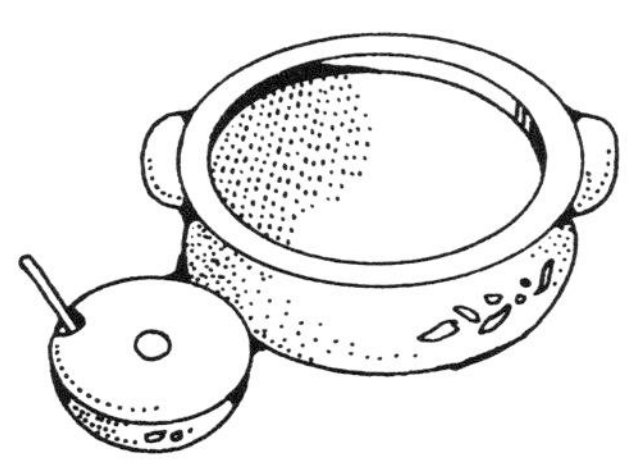

Long grain rice	2 cups (500 mL)
Butter	1/3 cup (75 mL)
Instant minced onion	2 Tbsp (25 mL)
Saffron	pinch, optional
Pepper	1/4 tsp (1 mL)
Chicken stock	4 cups (1 L), hot

1 Place rice in a strainer and rinse under cold running water until water is clear.

2 In a medium-sized skillet melt butter, add rice and cook, stirring constantly until rice takes on a light golden colour. Put in a 3-quart (3-L) casserole and set aside.

Last minute preparation Add onion, saffron and pepper to rice. Pour boiling stock into the casserole, stir, cover and bake at 350°F (180°C) for 50 minutes, or until all liquid has been absorbed and rice is tender. Fluff with a fork and serve.

SPINACH AND FRUIT SALAD

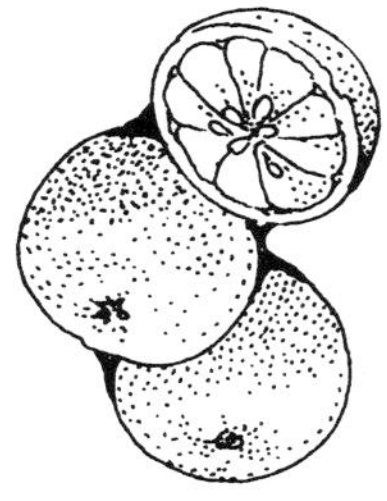

Fresh spinach	20 oz (560 g)
Oranges	3
Honeydew or cantaloupe melon	1 small
Onion	5 tsp (20 mL) grated
Salt	1/2 tsp (2 mL)
Pepper	1/4 tsp (1 mL)
Dry mustard	5 tsp (20 mL)
Lemon juice	1 1/2 tsp (7 mL)
Paprika	1 tsp (5 mL)
White wine vinegar	3 Tbsp (50 mL)
Honey	1 Tbsp (15 mL)
Olive oil	1 cup (250 mL)

1 Wash spinach, remove stems and tear into bite-sized pieces. Wrap in paper towels and store in plastic bag in refrigerator.

2 Peel and section oranges, removing any seeds. Seed melon and make melon balls. Store in refrigerator.

3 Make dressing by combining onion, salt, pepper, mustard, lemon juice, paprika, vinegar and honey. Slowly add olive oil, beating until thick. Store in a jar.

Last minute preparation Combine spinach, oranges and melon balls in a chilled salad bowl. Add dressing and toss thoroughly.

IRISH COFFEE MOUSSE

Fresh lemon	1/2
Water	1 cup (250 mL)
Unflavoured gelatin	1 envelope
Egg yolks	4
Sugar	3/4 cup (175 mL)
Instant coffee powder	2 Tbsp (25 mL)
Irish whiskey	2/3 cup (150 mL)
Cocoa	2 Tbsp (25 mL)
Whipping cream	3 cups (750 mL)
Icing sugar	2 Tbsp (25 mL)

1 Rub rims of 8 large Irish coffee or wine glasses with lemon, then twirl rims in a bowl of sugar. Set aside to dry.

2 Sprinkle gelatin over 1/4 cup (50 mL) water in a bowl and let set for 5 minutes.

3 In top of double boiler, beat yolks and sugar until lemon coloured, then add gelatin, remaining water and coffee powder. Cook over low heat until gelatin is dissolved. Remove from heat.

4 Combine 1/2 cup (125 mL) Irish whiskey and 1 Tbsp (15 mL) cocoa, then add to egg mixture. Set aside to cool.

5 Beat 2 cups (500 mL) whipping cream until stiff, then fold into cool gelatin mixture. Turn into prepared glasses and refrigerate.

6 Beat 1 cup (250 mL) cream until light, then add icing sugar and remaining 2 Tbsp (25 mL) whiskey and continue beating until stiff. Top each glass with whipped cream and sift remaining cocoa over the top.

Last minute preparation Serve cold with long handled spoons.

TIME AND TEMPERATURE CHART

8:10	350°F (180°C)	Quiche Tarts Water Chestnuts Savoury Rice
8:35	350°F (180°C)	Stuffed Zucchini
8:45	Stove top	Veal

Simple Gourmet Menu #7

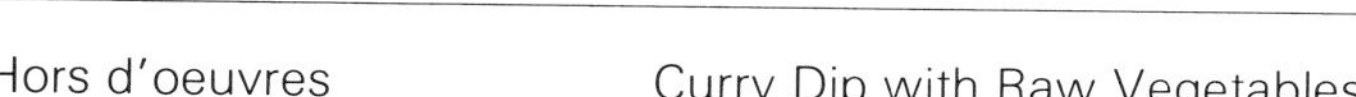

Hors d'oeuvres	Curry Dip with Raw Vegetables Teriyaki Meatballs
Main Course	Halibut or Swordfish Steaks Spiced Green Beans Crispy Squash Squares Spinach-Stuffed Baked Potatoes
Dessert	Coffee Gateau

Co-op Chart

Host/Hostess	Halibut or Swordfish Steaks
Couple A	Curry Dip, Stuffed Baked Potatoes
Couple B	Teriyaki Meatballs, Green Beans
Couple C	Squash Squares, Coffee Gateau

CURRY DIP WITH RAW VEGETABLES

Mayonnaise	1 cup (250 mL)
Horseradish	2 tsp (10 mL)
Onion	2 tsp (10 mL) grated
Curry powder	1 tsp (5 mL)
Salt	1 tsp (5 mL)
Raw vegetables — carrots, red or green pepper, green onions, cauliflower, zucchini, celery, broccoli, mushrooms, radishes	6 cups (1.5 L), assortment

1 Make dip by combining mayonnaise, horseradish, onion, curry and salt. Refrigerate.

2 Prepare raw vegetables by washing and cutting into bite-sized pieces. Keep crisp.

Last minute preparation Arrange vegetables on a platter and serve with dip.

TERIYAKI MEATBALLS

Soft bread crumbs	1 cup (250 mL)
Ground beef	1 lb (500 g)
Egg	1
Onion	1 Tbsp (15 mL) grated
Salt	1/2 tsp (2 mL)
Garlic	2 cloves
Fresh ginger	1 slice, size of a quarter
Soy sauce	3 Tbsp (50 mL)
Beef stock	1/2 cup (125 mL)
Molasses	2 Tbsp (25 mL)
Cornstarch	1 Tbsp (15 mL)
Water	2 Tbsp (25 mL)

1 Combine crumbs with ground beef, egg, grated onion and salt and form into small meatballs. Broil, turning once, until cooked and brown.

2 Mince garlic and ginger and add to soy sauce, stock and molasses in a large saucepan. Add meatballs, cover and simmer for 10 to 15 minutes.

3 Combine cornstarch and water and add to sauce. Cook, stirring for 2 to 3 minutes, then remove from heat. Cool and store in refrigerator.

Last minute preparation Reheat gently on stove top and serve with toothpicks.

HALIBUT OR SWORDFISH STEAKS

Olive oil	1 cup (250 mL)
Fresh parsley	3 Tbsp (50 mL) chopped
Dried oregano	1/2 tsp (2 mL)
Dried basil	1/2 tsp (2 mL)
Bay leaves	4
Green onions	2, chopped
Lemon juice	1/4 cup (50 mL)
Peppercorns	8, cracked
Halibut or swordfish steaks	10 medium
Flour	1 cup (250 mL)
Salt	1 tsp (5 mL)
Pepper	1 tsp (5 mL)
Lemons	2, cut in wedges

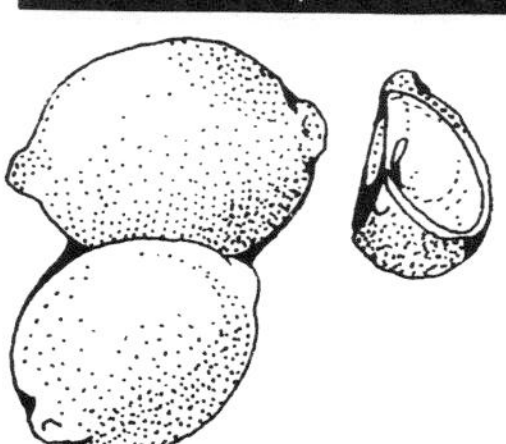

1 Prepare marinade by combining oil, parsley, oregano, basil, bay leaves, onions, lemon juice and peppercorns. Add fish and marinate for 2 hours, turning occasionally.

2 Remove fish from marinade and strain.

3 Combine flour with salt and pepper and dredge fish in flour. Heat marinade in a heavy skillet and brown fish lightly on both sides. Transfer to ovenproof casserole and reserve marinade. Cover and refrigerate.

Last minute preparation Bake, uncovered, at 350°F (180°C) for 20 to 25 minutes, basting frequently with pan juices or reserved marinade. The fish is done when it flakes easily. Test by inserting a table fork into the fish and giving it a slight twist. If fish breaks into flakes, it is cooked. Serve with lemon wedges.

SPICED GREEN BEANS

Fresh green beans	2 lbs (1 kg)
Salt	1 Tbsp (15 mL)
Oil	1 Tbsp (15 mL)
Garlic	1 large clove, minced
Onion	2 Tbsp (25 mL) chopped
Lemon juice	2 Tbsp (25 mL)
Brown sugar	1/4 cup (50 mL)
Bay leaf	1
Ground allspice	pinch

1 Wash beans, remove ends and cut diagonally. In a medium-sized pot, bring 2 quarts (2 L) water to a boil. Add 1 Tbsp (15 mL) salt and the beans. Return to the boil and cook, uncovered, for 5 minutes.

2 Drain and immediately plunge into cold water to stop cooking process. Drain again, cover and refrigerate.

3 In a skillet, heat oil and sauté garlic and onion until soft. Add lemon juice, sugar, bay leaf and allspice and set aside.

Last minute preparation In a saucepan combine beans, onion-spice mixture and 1/4 cup (50 mL) water. Heat over medium heat until warmed through. Remove bay leaf before serving.

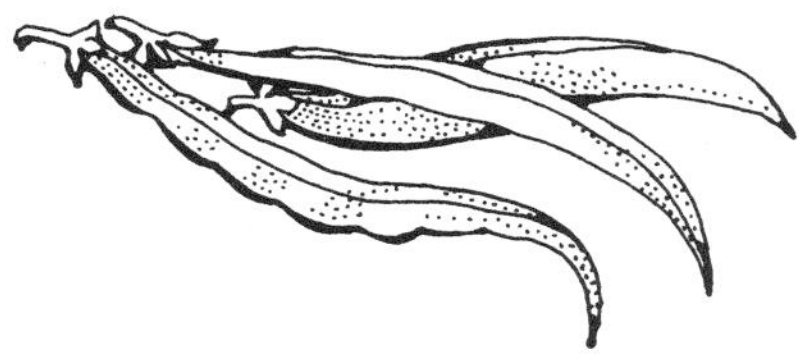

CRISPY SQUASH SQUARES

Hubbard squash	4 lbs (2 kg)
Walnut pieces	1/2 cup (125 mL)
Rice Krispies	1/2 cup (125 mL)
Brown sugar	1/3 cup (75 mL)
Pepper	1/2 tsp (2 mL)
Butter	2/3 cup (150 mL)

1. Cut squash in half, remove seeds and bake, covered, at 375°F (190°C) for 45 minutes, or until almost tender.
2. Cool and peel, then cut into 8 pieces.
3. Chop walnuts and crush Rice Krispies. Combine with brown sugar and pepper and set aside.
4. Melt butter and dip squash squares first in butter, then in nut mixture to coat completely. Arrange on a shallow baking pan and cover. Note: If preparing squash well in advance, do not coat with butter and nuts until shortly before final baking.

Last minute preparation Bake, covered, at 350°F (180°C) for 25 minutes. Uncover and bake 5 minutes more, or until lightly browned.

SPINACH-STUFFED BAKED POTATOES

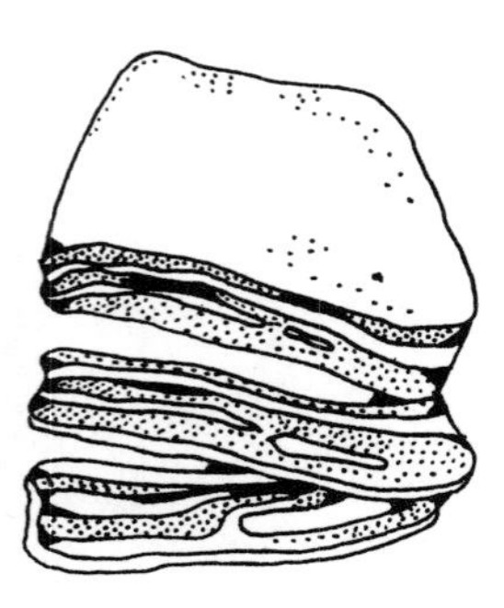

Baking potatoes	8 medium
Fresh spinach	10 oz (280 g)
Bacon	4 slices
Onion	1/3 cup (75 mL) finely chopped
Milk	1/3 cup (75 mL)
Butter	2 Tbsp (25 mL)
Egg	1 large
Pepper	1/4 tsp (1 mL)
Cheddar cheese	1 cup (250 mL) grated

1. Scrub potatoes, prick skin and bake at 425°F (220°C) for 50 to 60 minutes until soft.
2. Wash spinach, shake dry and cook in 1 Tbsp (15 mL) of water. Drain and chop.
3. Cook bacon until crisp; drain and crumble.
4. Cut a slice from the top of each potato and carefully scoop out pulp and mash. Add onion, milk, butter, egg, pepper, spinach and bacon and combine well. Spoon mixture back into shells and arrange on lightly greased baking sheet and refrigerate.

Last minute preparation Bake, uncovered, at 350°F (180°C) for 20 minutes. Sprinkle with cheese and return to oven for 10 more minutes.

COFFEE GATEAU

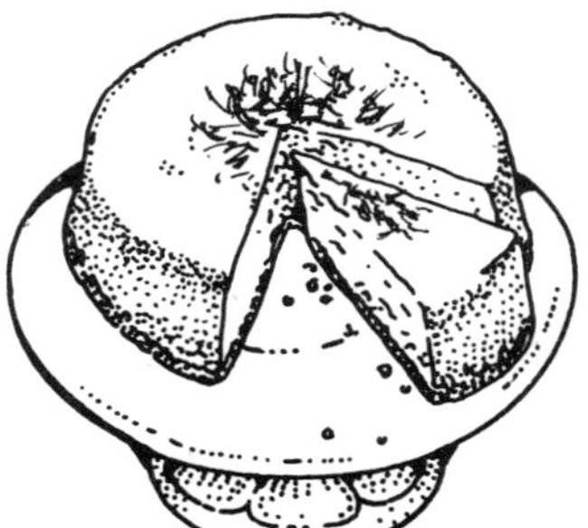

Lady fingers	12, split in half
Unflavoured gelatin	2 envelopes
Cold water	6 Tbsp (100 mL)
Egg yolks	5
Sugar	6 Tbsp (100 mL)
Milk	2 1/2 cups (625 mL)
Instant coffee powder	3 Tbsp (50 mL)
Coffee flavoured liqueur	1/4 cup (50 mL)
Whipping cream	1 1/2 cups (375 mL)
Icing sugar	2 Tbsp (25 mL)
Chocolate	1 oz (30 g)

1 Rub the inside of a large mold or bundt pan with butter and press the lady fingers onto the sides.

2 Add gelatin to water and soak for 5 minutes.

3 In the top of a double boiler beat egg yolks and sugar until thick and creamy. Add milk, coffee powder and gelatin mixture and cook over medium heat until custard is thick, stirring constantly. Remove from heat and add liqueur. Let mixture cool until it begins to set.

4 Whip 1 cup (250 mL) cream and fold into cooled custard. Turn into lined mold and refrigerate at least 4 hours.

5 Unmold the dessert onto a serving dish. Whip remaining 1/2 cup (125 mL) cream until stiff, adding icing sugar near the end. Decorate top of mold with whipped cream. Make chocolate shavings by scraping a knife or vegetable peeler across a piece of chocolate at room temperature. Decorate gateau with chocolate shavings and chill. Note: Mold may be prepared ahead of time, but should not be iced with whipped cream too far in advance.

Last minute preparation Store in refrigerator until serving time.

TIME AND TEMPERATURE CHART

8:10	Stove top	Meatballs
8:30	350°F (180°C)	Halibut or Swordfish Steaks
		Stuffed Baked Potatoes
		Squash Squares
8:50	Stove top	Green Beans

Gourmet Menus

#1	Hors d'oeuvres	Anchovy Tartlets
	First Course	Curried Vichyssoise
	Main Course	Amaretto Chicken Zucchini and Tomato Casserole Risotto French-Style Carrots
	Dessert	Chocolate Mousse Royale
#2	Hors d'oeuvres	Golden Cheddar Puffs
	First Course	Smoked Mussels Florentine
	Main Course	Crown Roast of Pork Sweet Potatoes and Cranberries Gourmet Green Peas Mushroom-Celery Salad
	Dessert	Banana Praline
#3	Hors d'oeuvres	Avocado Dip Piquant Chicken Tidbits
	First Course	Cream of Carrot Soup
	Main Course	Scampi Almond Rice Vegetable Potpourri
	Dessert	Glazed Apple-Walnut Flan
#4	Hors d'oeuvres	Crab Mousse
	First Course	Cream of Almond Soup
	Main Course	Beef Wellington Drambuie Yams Brussels Sprouts with Cashews Cauliflower, Tomato and Zucchini
	Dessert	Brandy Alexander Pie

#5	Hors d'oeuvres	Crab Meat-Stuffed Mushroom Caps
	First Course	Gazpacho
	Main Course	Stuffed Fillets of Sole Noodles Alfredo Atlanta Green Beans Saucy Beets
	Dessert	Chocolate Amaretto Cheesecake
#6	Hors d'oeuvres	Smoked Salmon Pâté
	First Course	Crème du Barry
	Main Course	Éstouffade de Boeuf Potatoes Romanoff Tomatoes Provençale Avocado and Grapefruit Salad
	Dessert	Grasshopper Pie
#7	Hors d'oeuvres	Caviar Mold Mushroom Pastries
	Main Course	Coq au Vin Parsley Potatoes Broccoli Soufflé Tomatoes Vinaigrette
	Dessert	Meringues with Apple Foam
#8	Hors d'oeuvres	Cheese Clouds Sweet and Sour Sausage Balls
	First Course	Chilled Tomato Consommé
	Main Course	Paella Savory Broccoli Orange and Green Salad
	Dessert	Mocha Coupes

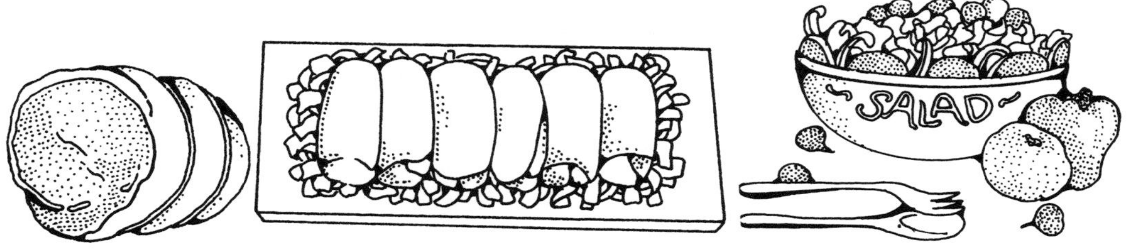

Gourmet Menu #1

Hors d'oeuvres	Anchovy Tartlets
First Course	Curried Vichyssoise
Main Course	Amaretto Chicken
	Zucchini Provençale
	Risotto
	French-Style Carrots
Dessert	Chocolate Mousse Royale

Co-op Chart

Host/Hostess	Amaretto Chicken
Couple A	Anchovy Tartlets, Zucchini Provençale
Couple B	Curried Vichyssoise, Risotto
Couple C	Carrots, Chocolate Mousse Royale

ANCHOVY TARTLETS

All-purpose flour	1 1/2 cups (375 mL) sifted
Dry mustard	1/8 tsp (0.5 mL)
Salt	1/8 tsp (0.5 mL)
Butter	3/4 cup (175 mL)
Shortening	2 Tbsp (25 mL)
Eggs	6
Whipping cream	1 cup (250 mL)
Pepper	1/8 tsp (0.5 mL)
Anchovy fillets	3 2-oz (50-g) cans

1 Sift flour, mustard and salt together and rub in butter and shortening. Add just enough water to form a dough that sticks together. Chill for 30 minutes.

2 Roll out pastry thinly and line two dozen 2-inch (5-cm) tart tins. Cover and refrigerate.

3 Beat eggs, cream and pepper. Drain anchovies and chop finely. Add to eggs and mix well. Cover and refrigerate.

Last minute preparation Stir anchovy mixture and spoon into tart tins. Bake at 400 °F (200 °C) for 12 to 15 minutes or until puffy and golden in colour.

CURRIED VICHYSSOISE

Leeks	4
Onion	1 medium
Potatoes	3 medium
Butter	4 Tbsp (65 mL)
Curry powder	1/8 tsp (0.5 mL)
Chicken stock	4 cups (1 L)
Salt	1/2 tsp (2 mL)
Pepper	1/2 tsp (2 mL)
Light cream	3 cups (750 mL)
Tabasco	dash
Fresh chives	2 Tbsp (25 mL) chopped

1 Wash leeks well and slice white and light green parts only. Peel and chop onion and potatoes.

2 Melt butter over medium heat and cook leeks and onion with curry powder until transparent, about 5 minutes. Do not brown.

3 Add potatoes, stock, salt and pepper and simmer until the potatoes are cooked, about 30 minutes.

4 Purée in blender or mash well by hand and push through fine sieve. Cool and refrigerate.

Last minute preparation Add the cream and Tabasco and stir well. Serve chilled in individual bowls garnished with chopped chives.

AMARETTO CHICKEN

Chicken breasts and/or legs	10 to 12 pieces
Flour	6 Tbsp (100 mL)
Salt	2 tsp (10 mL)
Pepper	1 tsp (5 mL)
Paprika	4 tsp (20 mL)
Vegetable oil	3 Tbsp (50 mL)
Butter	1/3 cup (75 mL)
Garlic	1 large clove, minced
Frozen orange juice concentrate	1 6 1/4-oz (178-mL) can, thawed
Dry mustard	3 Tbsp (50 mL)
Orange rind	1 tsp (5 mL) grated
Ground cloves	1/4 tsp (1 mL)
Dried thyme	1/4 tsp (1 mL)
Water	3/4 cup (175 mL)
Amaretto liqueur	1 1/2 cups (375 mL)
Seedless green grapes	1 1/2 cups (375 mL)
Toasted slivered almonds	1/2 cup (125 mL)

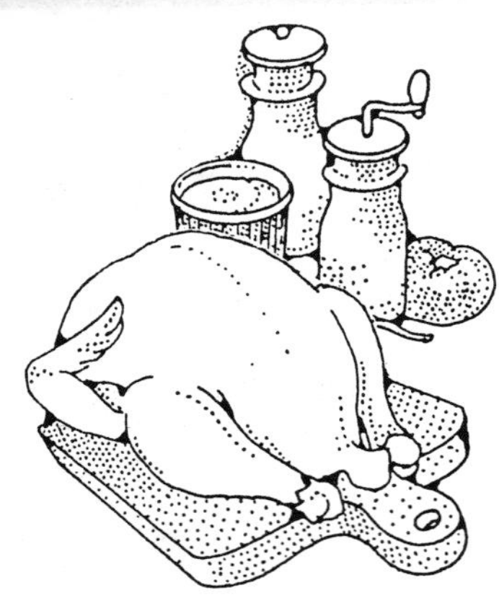

1 Combine flour, salt, pepper and paprika and coat the chicken by shaking in a bag. Reserve seasoned flour.

2 In heavy skillet heat oil and butter and sauté the chicken, a few pieces at a time, until brown on all sides. Cook dark meat 10 minutes longer than white, then place in ovenproof casserole.

3 To skillet add garlic and reserved flour. Cook for 2 minutes, then stir in orange juice. Add mustard, orange rind, cloves, thyme, water and Amaretto. Boil and stir until thickened.

4 Combine sauce and chicken pieces and bake, covered, at 350°F (180°C) for 40 minutes. Cool and refrigerate.

Last minute preparation Bake, covered, at 350°F (180°C) for 20 minutes, then add grapes and return to oven for 10 minutes. Place chicken pieces on serving plate. Pour sauce over and sprinkle with almonds.

ZUCCHINI PROVENÇALE

Tomatoes	3 lbs (1.5 kg)
Onions	2 large, chopped
Garlic	1 large clove, minced
Olive oil	6 Tbsp (100 mL)
Small zucchini	2 1/2 lbs (1.25 kg)
Dried thyme	1 tsp (5 mL)
Salt	1 1/2 tsp (7 mL)
Pepper	1 tsp (5 mL)
Parmesan cheese	1/2 cup (125 mL)

1 Remove the core from each tomato and cut into slices 1/2 inch (1.5 cm) thick.

2 Cook onions and garlic in 3 Tbsp (50 mL) oil until soft, but not brown. Add tomatoes and cook for 1 minute.

3 Wash zucchini and cut into 1/4-inch (5-mm) slices. Sauté in 3 Tbsp (50 mL) oil for 2 minutes.

4 Oil the bottom and sides of a 9-inch by 13-inch (3.5-L) casserole and arrange long rows of zucchini and tomatoes, forming alternating bands of red and green.

5 Combine thyme, salt, pepper and cheese and sprinkle over the dish. Cover and store in refrigerator.

Last minute preparation Bake, uncovered, at 350°F (180°C) for 40 minutes.

RISOTTO

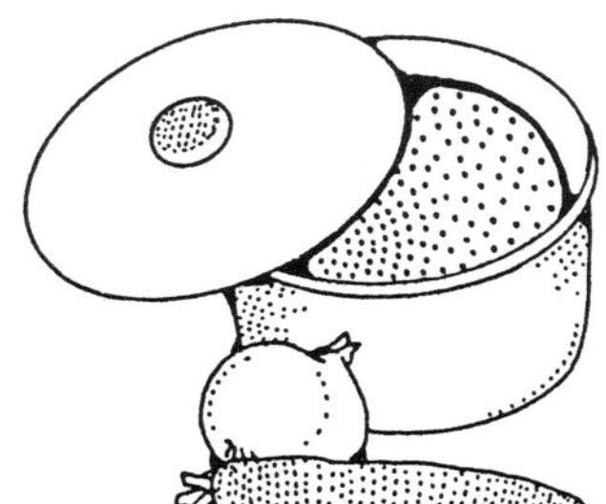

Long grain rice	2 cups (500 mL)
Butter	6 Tbsp (100 mL)
Onion	1/4 cup (50 mL) finely chopped
Ground nutmeg	1/4 tsp (1 mL)
White pepper	1/4 tsp (1 mL)
Dried basil	1/4 tsp (1 mL)
Salt	1 tsp (5 mL)
Bay leaves	2
Chicken stock	4 1/2 cups (1.125 L)
White wine	1/2 cup (125 mL)

1 Rinse rice under cold running water until water runs clear.

2 Melt 2 Tbsp (25 mL) butter and sauté onion until transparent, then add rice. Cook, stirring occasionally, until rice absorbs all the butter. Do not brown the rice.

3 Add nutmeg, pepper, basil, salt and bay leaves and slowly pour in 2 cups (500 mL) boiling stock, stirring until all the liquid is absorbed. Add remaining stock and wine, cover and cook for approximately 25 minutes.

4 Remove bay leaves, fluff with a fork and adjust the seasonings. Put in shallow baking pan, cover and refrigerate.

Last minute preparation Dot remaining 4 Tbsp (75 mL) butter over top of rice, cover and bake at 350°F (180°C) for 20 minutes. Fluff with a fork again before serving.

FRENCH-STYLE CARROTS

Carrots	2 lbs (1 kg)
Chicken stock	3/4 cup (175 mL)
Butter	1/4 cup (50 mL)
Salt	2 tsp (10 mL)
Pepper	1/2 tsp (2 mL)
Sugar	2 tsp (10 mL)
Lemon juice	2 tsp (10 mL)
Fresh parsley	1/4 cup (50 mL) chopped

1 Peel carrots and slice diagonally 1/4 inch (5 mm) thick. Store covered in water.

Last minute preparation Bring chicken stock to a boil and add butter, salt, pepper, sugar and drained carrots. Cover and simmer until carrots are just tender, about 10 to 15 minutes. Drain, add lemon juice and parsley and toss together.

CHOCOLATE MOUSSE ROYALE

Meringue

Icing sugar	1 cup (250 mL)
Ground filberts (hazelnuts)	1/4 cup (50 mL)
Egg whites	3
Almond extract	1/4 tsp (1 mL)
White sugar	1/3 cup (75 mL)

Mousse

Whipping cream	2 cups (500 mL)
Semi-sweet chocolate	6 oz (175 g)
Unsweetened chocolate	2 oz (60 g)
Egg whites	4
Vanilla extract	1/2 tsp (2 mL)
Almond extract	1/4 tsp (1 mL)

1 To make meringue, sift icing sugar and fold in ground filberts.

2 With an electric mixer beat egg whites and almond extract until stiff, then gradually add white sugar, 2 Tbsp (25 mL) at a time, while continuing to beat. Carefully fold in sugar and nut mixture.

3 Lightly oil a large cookie sheet. Spread meringue on sheet to form three 7-inch (17-cm) circles. Bake at 275°F (140°C) for 1 1/2 hours. When meringue is cooked, do not remove from oven, but turn off heat and open oven door and allow meringue to cool.

4 To make mousse, combine 1 cup (250 mL) cream and both chocolates in top of double boiler. Heat, stirring until chocolate is melted. Set aside to cool.

5 Beat egg whites until stiff and gently fold into cooled chocolate. Beat remaining 1 cup (250 mL) whipping cream with vanilla extract and almond extract until stiff. Fold into chocolate mixture.

6 To assemble, place one meringue on a serving plate and spread with a thin layer of mousse. Top with a second meringue and another thin layer of mousse. Top with last meringue and carefully ice top and sides with remaining mousse. Freeze for several hours.

Last minute preparation Thaw dessert in refrigerator for about 1/2 hour before serving.

TIME AND TEMPERATURE CHART

8:05	400°F (200°C)	Anchovy Tartlets
8:30	350°F (180°C)	Zucchini Provençale
8:40	350°F (180°C)	Amaretto Chicken
8:50	350°F (180°C)	Risotto
8:55	Stove top	Carrots

Gourmet Menu #2

Hors d'oeuvres	Golden Cheese Puffs
First Course	Smoked Mussels Florentine
Main Course	Crown Roast of Pork
	Sweet Potatoes and Cranberries
	Gourmet Green Peas
	Mushroom-Celery Salad
Dessert	Banana Praline

Co-op Chart

Host/Hostess	Crown Roast of Pork
Couple A	Cheese Puffs, Sweet Potatoes
Couple B	Smoked Mussels, Green Peas
Couple C	Mushroom-Celery Salad, Banana Praline

GOLDEN CHEESE PUFFS

Water	1 cup (250 mL)
Butter	1/2 cup (125 mL)
Salt	1/4 tsp (1 mL)
All-purpose flour	1 cup (250 mL)
Eggs	4
Sharp Cheddar cheese	1/2 cup (125 mL) shredded
Parmesan cheese	1/4 cup (50 mL) grated

1 In a medium-sized saucepan heat water, butter and salt to boiling. Add flour all at once, stirring over medium heat until mixture becomes smooth and leaves the sides of the pan. Remove from heat.

2 Add eggs, one at a time, beating well after each addition. Stir in Cheddar cheese.

3 Drop mixture by large spoonfuls 1 inch (2.5 cm) apart on greased baking sheet. Sprinkle with Parmesan cheese.

4 Bake at 400°F (200°C) until golden brown, 25 to 30 minutes. Pierce side of each puff with a sharp knife and bake 5 minutes longer. Cool on a rack, then put in an airtight container and refrigerate.

Last minute preparation Reheat, uncovered, at 350°F (180°C) for about 8 minutes. Serve hot.

SMOKED MUSSELS FLORENTINE

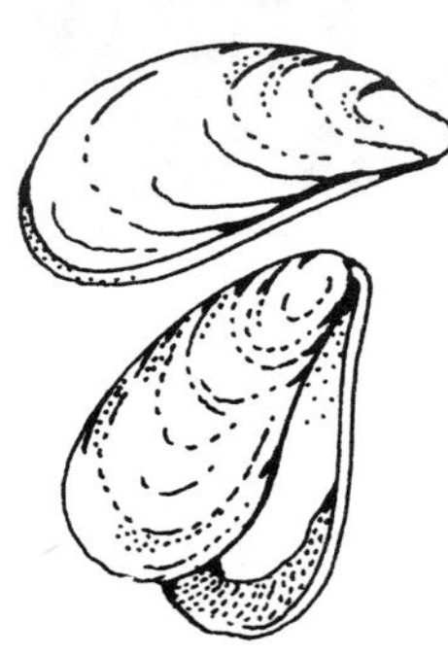

Fresh spinach	10 oz (280 g)
Green onions	2, chopped
Garlic	1 clove, minced
Fresh parsley	1/3 cup (75 mL) chopped
Butter	1/3 cup (75 mL) melted
Smoked mussels	2 3 3/4-oz (90-g) cans
Milk	1/2 cup (125 mL), approximately
Eggs	2
Pernod or anisette liqueur	1 Tbsp (15 mL), optional
Medium Cheddar cheese	1/2 cup (125 mL) grated
Dry bread crumbs	1/4 cup (50 mL)
Romano cheese	1/4 cup (50 mL) grated

1 Wash spinach, drain well and combine with onions, garlic and parsley.

2 In a medium-sized skillet melt 2 Tbsp (25 mL) butter and sauté the vegetables for 2 minutes.

3 Drain mussels. To their liquid add enough milk to equal 1/2 cup (125 mL) total liquid. Chop the mussels.

4 Lightly beat eggs, then add milk mixture, Pernod, spinach mixture, Cheddar cheese and mussels. Spoon mixture into 8 coquille shells or buttered 6-oz (175-mL) custard cups. Chill, covered.

5 Combine bread crumbs, Romano cheese and remaining butter. Store in a container.

Last minute preparation Sprinkle crumb mixture on top of each shell or cup. Bake at 350°F (180°C) for 15 to 20 minutes.

CROWN ROAST OF PORK

Pork loin roast	10 to 12 ribs
Salt	3 tsp (15 mL)
Pepper	1 1/2 tsp (7 mL)
Oranges	2 large
Sugar	3 Tbsp (50 mL)
Butter	1/2 cup (125 mL) melted
Soft bread crumbs	2 cups (500 mL)
Ground pork	1/2 lb (250 g)
Orange rind	1 Tbsp (15 mL) grated
Ground mace	1 tsp (5 mL)
Onion	2 Tbsp (25 mL) minced
Garlic	1 clove, minced
Whole spiced crab apples	1 14-oz (398-mL) jar

1 Have the butcher prepare crown by sawing vertebrae as usual and removing segments of meat between the ribs down to the loin. Bend the loin into a circle with rib ends pointing out and tie roast in this position with heavy string. Rub entire roast with 2 tsp (10 mL) salt and 1 tsp (5 mL) pepper and place on foil-covered shallow roasting pan. Wrap bone ends with foil to prevent excessive browning.

2 To make stuffing, peel and seed oranges and chop coarsely. In a large saucepan mix orange pulp with sugar, butter, bread crumbs, ground pork, orange rind, remaining salt and pepper, mace, onion and garlic. Cook over medium heat for 10 minutes, stirring. Cool and stuff inside of crown.

3 Insert meat thermometer so tip is in the thickest part of meat and does not rest on fat, bone or stuffing. Roast at 325°F (160°C), 30 to 35 minutes per pound (60 to 70 minutes per kg), or until thermometer reads 170°F (85°C).

Last minute preparation When roast is done, remove foil from bone ends and replace with red crab apples or paper frills. This is an impressive dish, so show it off in all its glory before carving. Spoon out the dressing into a serving dish and with the flourish of an expert just slice between each rib and serve.

SWEET POTATO AND CRANBERRY CASSEROLE

Sweet potatoes	6 large
Whole cranberry sauce	1 14-oz (398-mL) can
Rum	1/3 cup (75 mL)
Brown sugar	1/4 cup (50 mL)
Ground nutmeg	1/4 tsp (1 mL)
Butter	2 Tbsp (25 mL)
Cornstarch	1 Tbsp (15 mL)
Water	1/2 cup (125 mL)
Pecan pieces	1/2 cup (125 mL)

1 Boil sweet potatoes until tender. Cool, peel and slice, then place in a buttered 9-inch by 13-inch (3.5 L) casserole.

2 In a large saucepan combine cranberry sauce, rum, sugar, nutmeg and butter and boil. Combine cornstarch and water until smooth, then add to mixture. Lower heat and cook for 5 minutes, stirring frequently.

3 Pour sauce over potatoes in casserole and sprinkle with pecans. Cover and refrigerate.

Last minute preparation Bake, uncovered, in 350°F (180°C) oven for 30 minutes.

GOURMET GREEN PEAS

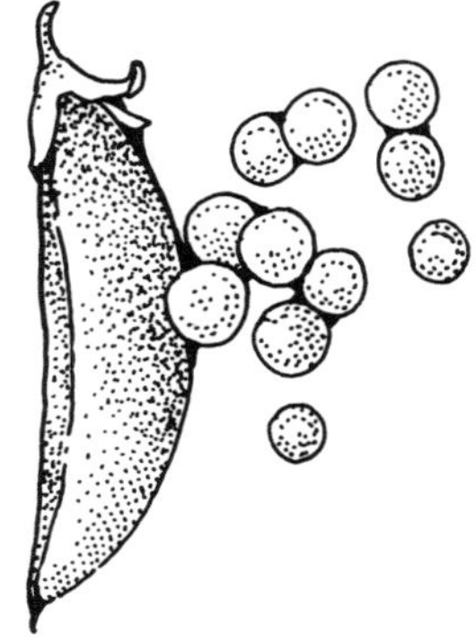

Frozen small green peas	20 oz (700 g)
Butter	6 Tbsp (100 mL)
Green onion	1, chopped
Sugar	1 tsp (5 mL)
Salt	1/2 tsp (2 mL)
Water	1/2 cup (125 mL)
Light cream	1/3 cup (75 mL)

Last minute preparation Combine peas, butter, green onion, sugar, salt and water in a saucepan and simmer until barely tender. Add cream and heat gently. Keep warm.

MUSHROOM-CELERY SALAD

Celery	1 large knob
Almonds	1/3 cup (75 mL)
Red onion	1/2 small, finely chopped
Lemon juice	2 Tbsp (25 mL)
Dry mustard	1 tsp (5 mL)
Salt	1/2 tsp (2 mL)
Dried tarragon	1/2 tsp (2 mL)
Pepper	1/4 tsp (1 mL)
Olive oil	1/3 cup (75 mL)
Fresh mushrooms	1/2 lb (250 g)
Fresh spinach	10 or 12 large leaves

1 Cut off root end of celery and wash well. Cut in thin crosswise slices, including leaves.

2 Toast almonds in middle of 350°F (180°C) oven, then grind or chop finely.

3 Combine onion, almonds, lemon juice, mustard, salt, tarragon and pepper. Add olive oil while continuing to mix. Pour over celery. Cover and refrigerate. Stir occasionally.

Last minute preparation Clean and slice mushrooms and add to celery mixture. Line small salad bowl with washed spinach leaves and mound salad mixture in the centre.

BANANA PRALINE

Sugar	1/2 cup (125 mL)
Cream of tartar	1/8 tsp (0.5 mL)
Water	1 Tbsp (15 mL)
Pecan pieces	1 cup (250 mL)
Yogurt or sour cream	1 1/2 cups (375 mL)
Butter	1/3 cup (75 mL)
Brown sugar	1/3 cup (75 mL)
Lemon juice	3 Tbsp (50 mL)
Grand Marnier	1/3 cup (75 mL)
Bananas	8

1 Oil a large baking sheet for cooling of praline syrup.

2 In a small heavy saucepan, combine sugar, cream of tartar and water. Stirring until sugar dissolves, boil over medium heat until mixture becomes a medium brown, 6 to 8 minutes. Do not let it get too dark.

3 Add pecans and pour mixture onto greased baking sheet in a thin layer. Cool.

4 Pulverize praline in a blender or food processor. Store in an airtight container.

Last minute preparation Stir praline powder into yogurt or sour cream. Heat a chafing dish and melt butter. Stir in brown sugar, lemon juice and Grand Marnier. Peel bananas and split lengthwise. Add to hot syrup and cook until heated through, about 5 minutes. Baste frequently with syrup, being careful not to overcook. Serve bananas on individual plates, each topped with some syrup and a spoonful of praline cream.

TIME AND TEMPERATURE CHART

Time	Temperature	Item
6:30	325°F (160°C)	Crown Roast of Pork
8:05	350°F (180°C)	Increase temperature, leave roast in
8:10	350°F (180°C)	Cheese Puffs
8:40	350°F (180°C)	Sweet Potatoes and Cranberries Smoked Mussels Florentine
8:55	Stove top	Gourmet Green Peas

Gourmet Menu #3

Hors d'oeuvres	Avocado Dip
	Piquant Chicken Tidbits
First Course	Cream of Carrot Soup
Main Course	Scampi
	Almond Rice
	Vegetable Potpourri
Dessert	Glazed Apple-Walnut Flan

Co-op Chart

Host/Hostess	Scampi
Couple A	Avocado Dip, Cream of Carrot Soup
Couple B	Chicken Tidbits, Vegetable Potpourri
Couple C	Almond Rice, Apple-Walnut Flan

Note Because of the high cost of scampi, a small contribution from each guest couple may be necessary.

AVOCADO DIP

Avocados	3 ripe
Onion	1 small, finely chopped
Tomatoes	2
Bacon	4 slices
Lemon juice	2 Tbsp (25 mL)
Salt	1/2 tsp (2 mL)
Tortilla chips	1 7-oz (200-g) package

1 Peel and pit the avocados and mash. Peel and seed tomatoes and chop finely. Cook bacon until crisp and crumble.

2 Combine avocado, onion, tomatoes, lemon juice and salt. Put one avocado pit in the bottom of a serving dish and add avocado mixture. Cover tightly and refrigerate. This dip should be prepared no more than 1 hour ahead since the avocados will darken if made too early. The presence of the pit will help slow down the darkening process.

Last minute preparation Remove pit, stir and serve with tortilla chips.

PIQUANT CHICKEN TIDBITS

Boned chicken breasts	3 single
Egg	1
Water	1 cup (250 mL)
All-purpose flour	1 1/2 cups (375 mL)
Salt	1 tsp (5 mL)
Oil	2 cups (500 mL)
Vinegar	1/4 cup (50 mL)
Peach, apricot or pineapple jam	1 cup (250 mL)
Fresh ginger	1 tsp (5 mL) grated
Chili powder	1/2 tsp (2 mL)
Orange juice	1 cup (250 mL)
Cornstarch	2 Tbsp (25 mL)
Water	2 Tbsp (25 mL)

1 Remove skin from chicken breasts and cut into 1-inch (2.5-cm) strips.

2 Prepare batter by beating together egg, 2 Tbsp (25 mL) oil and water. Add flour and salt and mix just until combined.

3 In a deep pot heat oil to 375°F (190°C). Dip chicken pieces into batter and drop into hot oil. Deep fry until golden brown. Drain on paper towels and continue until all chicken is cooked. Store, covered, in refrigerator.

4 In saucepan combine vinegar, jam, ginger, chili powder and orange juice and heat over medium heat until smooth.

5 Combine cornstarch with water until smooth, then add to sauce and cook, stirring constantly until thickened. Remove from heat and cool.

Last minute preparation Reheat chicken tidbits in 350°F (180°C) oven until hot, about 10 minutes. Meanwhile heat sauce on stove top. Combine sauce and chicken tidbits and serve with toothpicks.

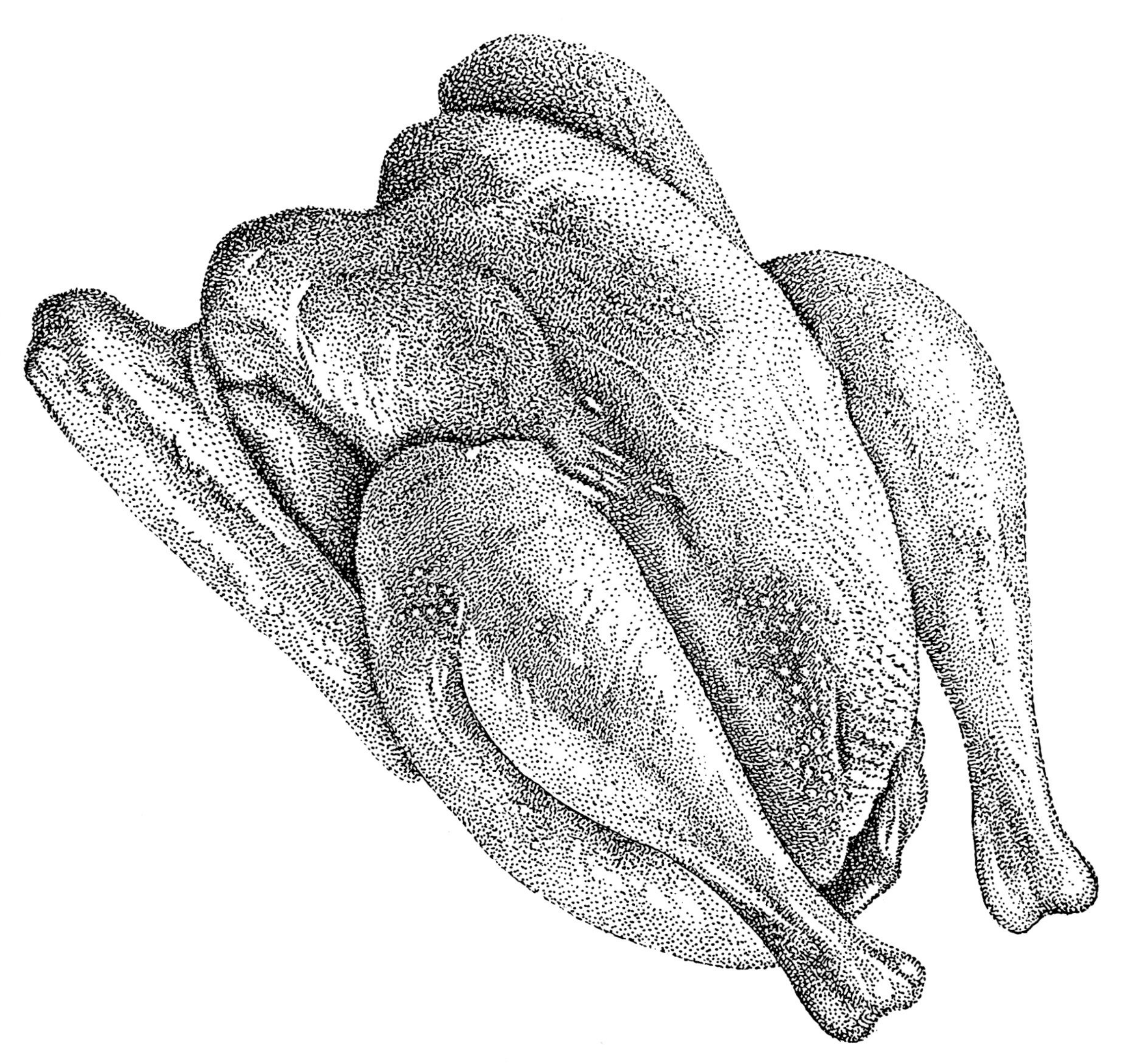

CREAM OF CARROT SOUP

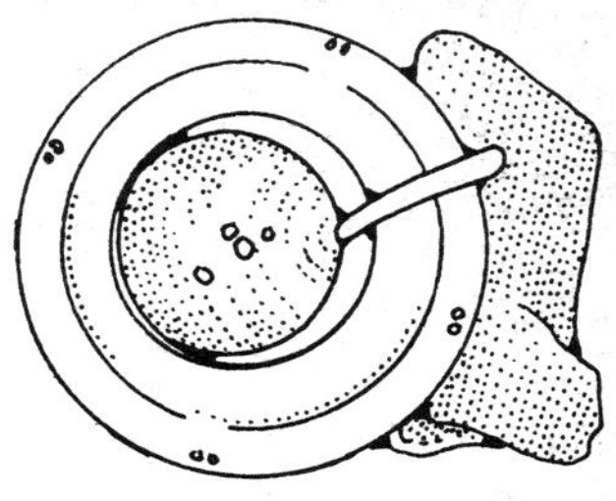

Butter	3 Tbsp (50 mL)
Onions	2 medium, sliced
Carrots	2 lbs (1 kg), peeled and sliced
Dill seeds	1/2 tsp (2 mL)
Chicken stock	5 cups (1.25 L)
Salt	1 tsp (5 mL)
Pepper	1/4 tsp (1 mL)
Ground nutmeg	1/8 tsp (0.5 mL)
Light cream	2 cups (500 mL)
Sour cream	1/2 cup (125 mL)
Fresh parsley	8 sprigs

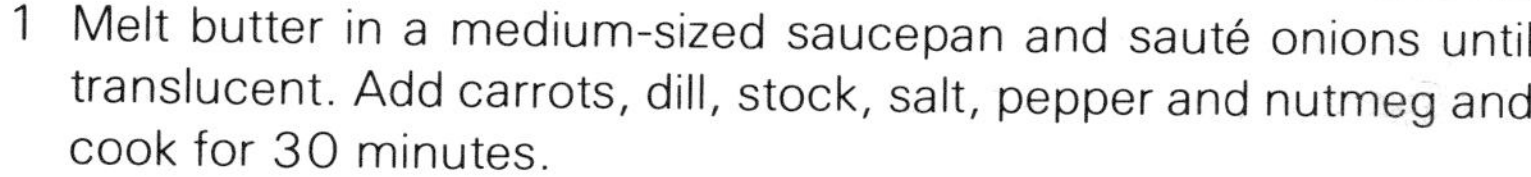

1 Melt butter in a medium-sized saucepan and sauté onions until translucent. Add carrots, dill, stock, salt, pepper and nutmeg and cook for 30 minutes.

2 Purée mixture, one third at a time, in blender or food processor. Chill thoroughly.

Last minute preparation Stir light cream into carrot mixture. Serve cold in individual bowls and garnish each with a spoonful of sour cream topped with a sprig of parsley.

SCAMPI

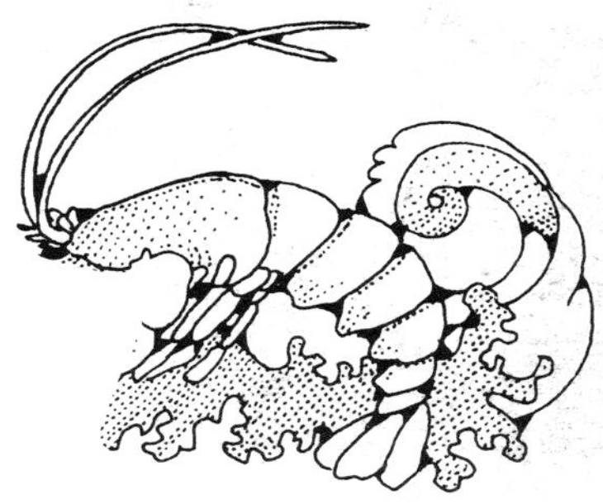

Unshelled scampi	4 lbs (2 kg)
Garlic butter	1/2 lb (250 g)
Dry bread crumbs	1 cup (250 mL), approximately

1 Defrost scampi if necessary. Lay scampi on its back curling upwards. Cut two slits to remove membrane; this will expose part of the meat.

2 Place scampi on cookie sheets with shell side down. Brush exposed part of each scampi with melted garlic butter and sprinkle bread crumbs on top.

Last minute preparation Broil for 3 to 5 minutes until golden and serve immediately. Serve extra melted garlic butter if desired.

Clockwise: Stuffed Fillet of Sole, in silver serving dish (page 78); Crab Meat-Stuffed Mushroom Caps (page 76); Saucy Beets (page 80); Chocolate Amaretto Cheesecake (page 81).

ALMOND RICE

Long grain rice	1 cup (250 mL)
Salt	1/2 tsp (2 mL)
Butter	1/3 cup (75 mL)
Garlic salt	1 tsp (5 mL)
Chicken stock	1 3/4 cups (425 mL)
Fresh parsley	2 Tbsp (25 mL) chopped
Slivered almonds	1/4 cup (50 mL)

1 Put rice and salt in a medium-sized pot and add enough boiling water to cover. Let stand 30 minutes, then rinse with cold water and drain.

2 Melt butter in a medium-sized skillet, add rice and sauté over medium heat for 5 minutes.

3 Place rice in 1-quart (1-L) casserole, add stock and sprinkle with garlic salt. Cover and refrigerate.

4 Toast almonds in a 350°F (180°C) oven until light golden in colour.

Last minute preparation Put casserole on stove top and bring contents to a boil. Cover and bake in oven at 350°F (180°C) for 45 to 50 minutes. Add finely chopped parsley and almonds just before serving.

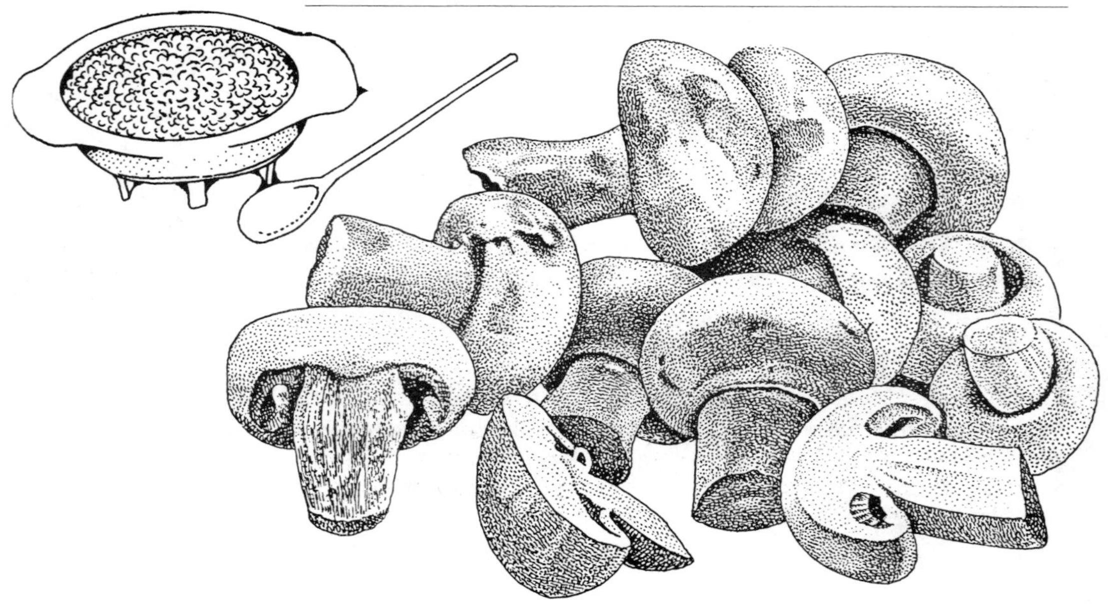

VEGETABLE POTPOURRI

Carrots	2 medium
Green beans	1/2 lb (250 g)
Celery	3 ribs
Cauliflower	1 medium head
Water	1 Tbsp (15 mL)
Cornstarch	1 1/2 tsp (7 mL)
Soy sauce	2 Tbsp (25 mL)
Dry sherry	1 Tbsp (15 mL)
Sugar	1 Tbsp (15 mL)
Pepper	1/8 tsp (0.5 mL)
Sweet red pepper	1
Fresh mushrooms	1/2 lb (250 g)
Onion	1 medium
Peanut or corn oil	3 Tbsp (50 mL)
Fresh ginger	1 tsp (5 mL) grated
Snow peas	24

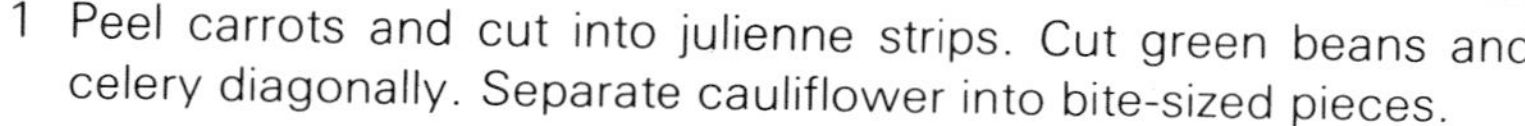

1 Peel carrots and cut into julienne strips. Cut green beans and celery diagonally. Separate cauliflower into bite-sized pieces.

2 In a large pot boil 2 cups (500 mL) salted water. Add carrots and green beans and cook for 3 minutes. Add cauliflower and celery and cook for 2 minutes longer.

3 Drain well, then plunge into ice cold water to stop cooking process. Drain again, cover and store in refrigerator.

4 Combine water, cornstarch, soy sauce, sherry, sugar and pepper. Store in a separate container.

5 Seed red pepper and cut into chunks. Clean and slice mushrooms. Store these vegetables together.

6 Peel and slice onion. Store separately.

Last minute preparation Preheat wok or large heavy saucepan over high heat, add oil, ginger and onions and sauté for 1 minute. Add carrots, beans, cauliflower, celery, red pepper and mushrooms and cook for 2 minutes longer until just tender. Add soy mixture and snow peas; cook for 3 to 4 minutes, stirring until sauce thickens.

GLAZED APPLE-WALNUT FLAN

Crust

All-purpose flour	1 1/2 cups (375 mL) sifted
Brown sugar	1/3 cup (75 mL)
Walnut pieces	1/4 cup (50 mL) finely chopped
Eggs	2 small
Salt	1/2 tsp (2 mL)
Vanilla extract	1/2 tsp (2 mL)
Butter	1/3 cup (75 mL), softened

Filling

Egg yolks	4
Brown sugar	1/2 cup (125 mL)
Flour	1 Tbsp (15 mL)
Light cream	2 cups (500 mL)
Vanilla extract	1/2 tsp (2 mL)
Tart apples	5 large
Cinnamon	1 tsp (5 mL)
Butter	1/3 cup (75 mL)
Brandy	3 Tbsp (50 mL)
Port	1/2 cup (125 mL)
Walnut pieces	1/2 cup (125 mL)
Unflavoured gelatin	1 tsp (5 mL)
Sugar	1/3 cup (75 mL)
Whipping cream	1 cup (250 mL)
Icing sugar	2 Tbsp (25 mL)

1 To make crust, mix flour, sugar and walnuts. Add eggs, salt, vanilla and soft butter and blend together until crumbly.

2 Line the bottom and 1 1/2 inches (4 cm) up the sides of a 9-inch (3-L) spring-form pan. Bake at 325°F (160°C) for 12 minutes. Cool.

3 To make filling, beat egg yolks and brown sugar with an electric mixer. Add flour, cream and vanilla and beat well. Pour into top of double boiler and cook over hot water until thickened. Pour into crust and bake at 350°F (180°C) for 20 to 30 minutes, or until set. Cool.

4 Peel, core and cut apples into eighths. In a medium-sized pot heat cinnamon, butter, 2 Tbsp (25 mL) brandy and 1/4 cup (50 mL) port. Add apples and cook, just until they begin to soften but still retain their shape, about 5 minutes.

5 Remove apples from liquid with a slotted spoon and arrange in a concentric circle pattern on top of the custard. Sprinkle walnuts over the apples and refrigerate flan.

6 In a small pot heat gelatin, sugar and 1/2 cup (125 mL) water until gelatin dissolves. Remove from heat and add 1/4 cup (50 mL) port. Cool until it just begins to set. Spoon gelatin mixture over apples. Cover and refrigerate flan.

7 Combine whipping cream and 1 Tbsp (15 mL) brandy. Whip until slightly stiff, then add icing sugar gradually and continue beating until stiff. Garnish flan with whipped cream. Note: Do not whip cream too far in advance.

Last minute preparation Remove from refrigerator 30 minutes before dessert time. Serve with a flourish and possibly a snifter of the same brandy.

TIME AND TEMPERATURE CHART

8:10	350°F (180°C)	Piquant Chicken Tidbits
8:15	Stove top	Piquant Sauce
8:20	350°F (180°C)	Rice
8:50	Stove top	Vegetable Potpourri
9:10		Remove rice from oven
9:10	Broil	Scampi

Gourmet Menu #4

Hors d'oeuvres	Crab Mousse
First Course	Cream of Almond Soup
Main Course	Beef Wellington
	Drambuie Yams
	Brussels Sprouts with Cashews
	Cauliflower, Tomatoes and Zucchini
Dessert	Brandy Alexander Pie

Co-op Chart

Host/Hostess	Beef Wellington
Couple A	Crab Mousse, Cauliflower, Tomatoes and Zucchini
Couple B	Almond Soup, Drambuie Yams
Couple C	Brussels Sprouts, Brandy Alexander Pie

Note Because of the high cost of the meat, a small contribution from each of the guest couples may be necessary.

CRAB MOUSSE

THYME

Crab meat	1 6-oz (170-g) can
Unflavoured gelatin	1 envelope
Water	1/2 cup (125 mL)
Condensed clam chowder	1 10-oz (284-mL) can
Cream cheese	8 oz (250 mL)
Celery	1/2 cup (125 mL) finely chopped
Green onions	1/2 cup (125 mL) finely chopped
Dried thyme	1 tsp (5 mL)
Mayonnaise	1 cup (250 mL)
Cayenne pepper	pinch
Pimento	2 tsp (10 mL) chopped
Crackers	assortment

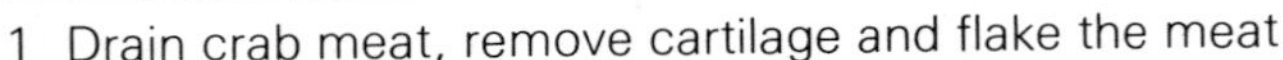

1 Drain crab meat, remove cartilage and flake the meat.

2 Sprinkle gelatin over cold water and let stand for 5 minutes to soften. Combine with soup and cream cheese and heat, stirring until smooth. Add crab meat, celery, onions, thyme, mayonnaise, cayenne and pimento and mix again.

3 Put mixture into oiled 3-cup (1-L) mold. Cover and refrigerate.

Last minute preparation Unmold mousse and serve cold with crackers.

CREAM OF ALMOND SOUP

Potato	1 medium
Green onions	4
Chicken stock	6 cups (1.5 L)
Bay leaf	1
Ground almonds	4 oz (125 g)
Pepper	1/8 tsp (0.5 mL)
Almond extract	1/4 tsp (1 mL)
Light cream	1 1/2 cups (375 mL)
Cornstarch	1 Tbsp (15 mL)
Ground nutmeg	1/8 tsp (0.5 mL)
Slivered almonds	1/3 cup (75 mL)

1 Peel potato and chop into medium-sized pieces. Chop white part only of green onions.

2 In a large pot bring chicken stock to a boil and add potatoes, onions, bay leaf, ground almonds and pepper. Cover and simmer for 30 minutes.

3 Remove bay leaf, add almond extract and 1 1/4 cups (300 mL) cream. Process until smooth in blender or food processor or mash by hand and push through a fine sieve.

4 Combine 1/4 cup (50 mL) cream, cornstarch and nutmeg and add to potato mixture. Reheat, stirring until thickened, but do not boil. Cool and refrigerate.

5 Put slivered almonds in a pan and bake at 350°F (180°C) until toasted, about 8 minutes. Cool.

Last minute preparation Reheat soup, being careful that it does not boil. Serve in heated bowls and garnish with toasted almonds. In summer this soup may be served chilled and garnished with chopped chives.

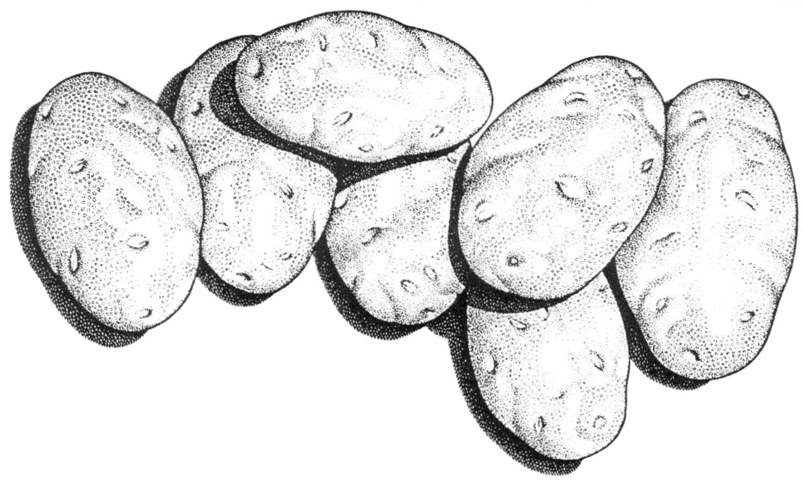

BEEF WELLINGTON

Frozen puff pastry	2 14-oz (397-g) packages
Beef tenderloin filet	3 lbs (1.5 kg)
Pepper	1/2 tsp (2 mL)
Brandy	2 Tbsp (25 mL)
Bacon	4 slices
Liver pâté	1/2 cup (125 mL)
Egg	1, beaten

1 Thaw puff pastry.

2 One hour before guests arrive, rub meat with pepper and brandy. Lay bacon over top of meat and roast at 450°F (230°C) for 20 minutes.

3 Remove from oven and cool to room temperature.

4 Remove bacon and reserve. Spread pâté evenly over top and sides of meat, then replace bacon.

5 Roll pastry to a size that will completely cover the tenderloin. Lay the cool meat in the centre and fold pastry around it, overlapping edges and folding the ends over. Be careful that the pastry does not break.

6 Transfer wrapped meat to a baking sheet, seam side down.

7 Decorate with leaves made from left-over pastry and cut two steam vents in the top. Glaze top of pastry with beaten egg.

Last minute preparation Thirty minutes before serving time, place beef in centre of a preheated 425°F (220°C) oven and bake for 15 minutes. Reduce heat to 400°F (200°C) and bake for 15 more minutes. Bring this masterpiece to the table for display before carving.

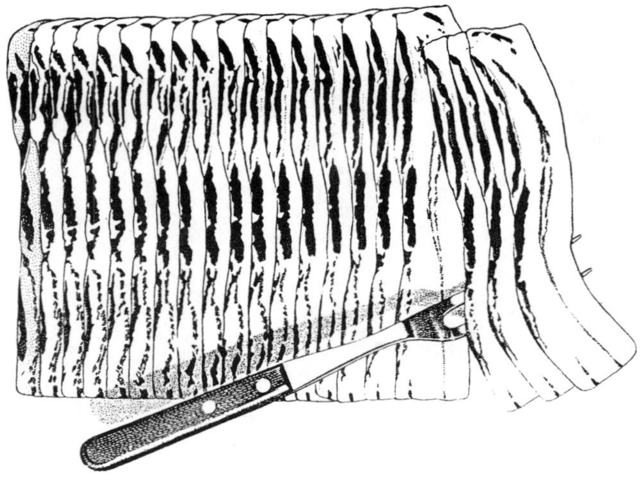

DRAMBUIE YAMS

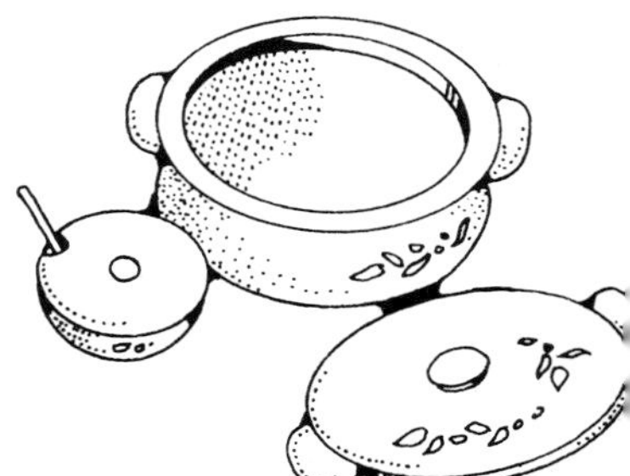

Yams or sweet potatoes	8 medium
Butter	1/3 cup (75 mL)
Brown sugar	6 Tbsp (100 mL)
Water	3 Tbsp (50 mL)
Honey	1/3 cup (75 mL)
Ground nutmeg	1/2 tsp (2 mL)
Drambuie liqueur	6 Tbsp (100 mL)

1 Wash potatoes, prick skin and arrange in an oiled baking dish. Bake at 350°F (180°C) (with a pan of water on the bottom rack to add moisture) until they are tender but not soft, about 1 hour. Cool.

2 Peel potatoes and cut in half. Arrange halves in ovenproof casserole.

3 In a small saucepan heat butter, sugar, water, honey, nutmeg and 3 Tbsp (50 mL) Drambuie until sugar has dissolved. Pour over potatoes in the casserole. Cover and refrigerate.

Last minute preparation Pour 3 Tbsp (50 mL) Drambuie over potatoes and bake, covered, at 400°F (200°C) for 15 minutes.

BRUSSELS SPROUTS WITH CASHEWS

Flour	3 Tbsp (50 mL)
Water	1 2/3 cups (400 mL)
Milk	1 cup (250 mL)
Salt	1 tsp (5 mL)
Dried thyme	1/4 tsp (1 mL)
Butter	3 Tbsp (50 mL)
Brussels sprouts	1 1/2 lbs (750 g)
Unsalted roasted cashew nuts	1 cup (250 mL)

1 In a small saucepan blend flour with 1/3 cup (75 mL) water until mixture is smooth. Add remaining water, milk, salt and thyme. Cook over medium heat and bring to a boil. Lower heat, add butter and cook until slightly thickened. Cool, cover and refrigerate.

2 Wash brussels sprouts, trim tough outer leaves and stems and cut an X into bottom of each stem to promote quick cooking. Drain well and set aside.

Last minute preparation Cook brussels sprouts, uncovered, in 1 inch (2.5 cm) salted water for 10 to 15 minutes. In top of double boiler gently reheat sauce, stirring constantly. Drain sprouts and toss with sauce and cashew nuts. Keep warm.

CAULIFLOWER, TOMATOES AND ZUCCHINI

Cauliflower	1 large head
Parmesan cheese	1 cup (250 mL) grated
Butter	3 Tbsp (50 mL)
Garlic	1 clove, minced
Onions	2, chopped
Zucchini	1 1/2 cups (375 mL) grated
Fresh parsley	2 Tbsp (25 mL) chopped
Tomatoes	1 19-oz (540-mL) can
Soy sauce	1 Tbsp (15 mL)
Sugar	1 Tbsp (15 mL)
Salt	1 tsp (5 mL)
Pepper	1/4 tsp (1 mL)
Dry bread crumbs	1/3 cup (75 mL)

1 Wash cauliflower and cut into florets. Cook in 1 inch (2.5 cm) boiling salted water for 5 minutes. Drain, return to pot and sprinkle with 3/4 cup (175 mL) cheese.

2 In a medium-sized frying pan melt butter and sauté garlic, onions and zucchini for 4 minutes. Add parsley, tomatoes with their liquid, soy sauce, sugar, salt, pepper and bread crumbs and simmer for 5 minutes.

3 Place half of tomato mixture in buttered 2-quart (2-L) casserole and add all the cauliflower-cheese mixture. Add remaining tomato mixture and sprinkle remaining 1/4 cup (50 mL) cheese over top. Cover and bake for 15 minutes at 350°F (180°C). Cool and refrigerate.

Last minute preparation Bake, uncovered, at 400°F (200°C) for 15 minutes.

BRANDY ALEXANDER PIE

Crust

Graham wafer crumbs	1 cup (250 mL)
Ground almonds	1/2 cup (125 mL)
Sugar	1/3 cup (75 mL)
Butter	1/3 cup (75 mL) melted

Filling

Unflavoured gelatin	1 envelope
Water	1/4 cup (50 mL)
Sugar	2/3 cup (150 mL)
Salt	1/8 tsp (0.5 mL)
Eggs	3, separated
Brandy	1/3 cup (75 mL)

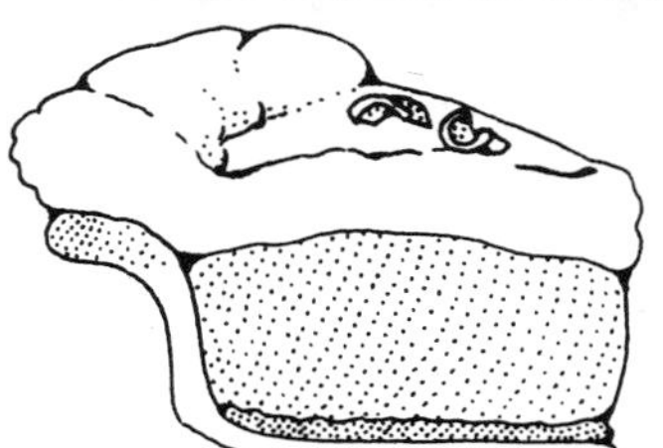

Crème de cacao liqueur	1/3 cup (75 mL)
Whipping cream	2 cups (500 mL)
Unsweetened chocolate	1 oz (30 g)

Note This dessert is best prepared 24 hours in advance to allow the filling to set. However, do not whip cream for garnish too far in advance.

1 To make crust, combine graham wafer crumbs, ground almonds, sugar and melted butter. Press into bottom of 9-inch (3-L) spring-form pan. Bake at 350°F (180°C) for 8 minutes. Cool.

2 To make filling, combine gelatin, 1/3 cup (75 mL) sugar, salt and cold water in top of double boiler. Heat over boiling water until gelatin is dissolved. Beat egg yolks and add gradually to gelatin mixture. Cook over boiling water until mixture thickens. Remove from heat, cool slightly, and stir in brandy and crème de cacao.

3 Beat egg whites until foamy and gradually add remaining 1/3 cup (75 mL) sugar, beating until stiff. Carefully fold gelatin mixture into egg whites.

4 Whip 1 cup (250 mL) cream until stiff and fold into brandy mixture. Pour filling into crust and chill for 24 hours.

5 Whip remaining cream until stiff and garnish the pie. Make chocolate curls by running a knife or vegetable peeler over chocolate at room temperature and sprinkle over pie.

Last minute preparation Remove spring-form pan and place this delectable pie on an attractive serving plate.

TIME AND TEMPERATURE CHART

8:40	425°F (220°C)	Beef Wellington
8:45	Stove top	Brussels Sprouts
8:50	Stove top	Cream of Almond Soup
8:55	400°F (200°C)	Reduce oven temperature, leave beef in oven Drambuie Yams Cauliflower, Tomatoes and Zucchini

Gourmet Menu #5

Hors d'oeuvres	Crab Meat-Stuffed Mushroom Caps
First Course	Gazpacho
Main Course	Stuffed Fillets of Sole
	Noodles Alfredo
	Atlanta Green Beans
	Saucy Beets
Dessert	Chocolate Amaretto Cheesecake

Co-op Chart

Host/Hostess	Stuffed Fillets of Sole
Couple A	Stuffed Mushrooms, Green Beans
Couple B	Gazpacho, Saucy Beets
Couple C	Noodles Alfredo, Chocolate Amaretto Cheesecake

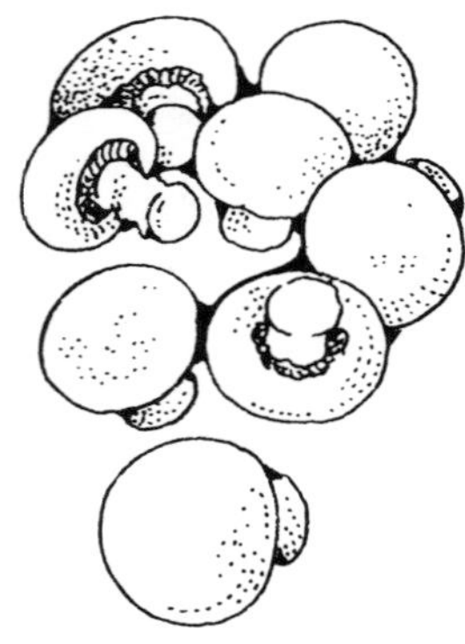

CRAB MEAT-STUFFED MUSHROOM CAPS

Crab meat	1 6-oz (170-g) can
Egg	1
Butter	4 Tbsp (50 mL)
Onion	1/3 cup (75 mL) finely chopped
Soft bread crumbs	3/4 cup (175 mL)
Worcestershire sauce	1 tsp (5 mL)
Cayenne pepper	pinch
Mushrooms	24 large
Dry bread crumbs	1/3 cup (75 mL)

1 Drain crab meat, remove any cartilage or shell and flake the meat. Mix in egg and set aside.

2 In a medium-sized frying pan melt 2 Tbsp (25 mL) butter and fry onions until transparent. Add soft bread crumbs, Worcestershire sauce and cayenne. Add to crab mixture, combine well and set aside.

3 Wipe mushrooms with a damp cloth and remove stems. Fill with crab mixture.

4 Melt 2 Tbsp (25 mL) butter and add dry bread crumbs. Sprinkle on top of stuffed mushrooms. Place mushrooms in a shallow baking dish and store, covered, in refrigerator.

Last minute preparation Broil until warm and crumbs are browned, 5 to 8 minutes. Serve hot.

GAZPACHO

Tomatoes	2 lbs (1 kg)
Cucumbers	2 small, chopped
Green pepper	1 cup (250 mL) chopped
Onions	2 small, chopped
Garlic	1 clove, minced
Fresh parsley	1/4 cup (50 mL)
Lemon juice	3 Tbsp (50 mL)
Tabasco sauce	1/8 tsp (0.5 mL)
Salt	1 tsp (5 mL)
Pepper	1/2 tsp (2 mL)
Tomato juice	2 cups (500 mL)
Beef stock	1 cup (250 mL)
Olive oil	3 Tbsp (50 mL)
Croutons	1 cup (250 mL)

1 Peel and seed tomatoes. Set aside half of the cucumber, pepper and onions.

2 In a food processor or blender, purée tomatoes, garlic, parsley and the remaining cucumber, green pepper and onions. Add lemon juice, Tabasco, salt and pepper, tomato juice, stock and oil.

3 Place in a large container, add reserved vegetables and mix. Chill thoroughly.

Last minute preparation Stir well and serve in chilled soup bowls, garnished with croutons.

STUFFED FILLETS OF SOLE

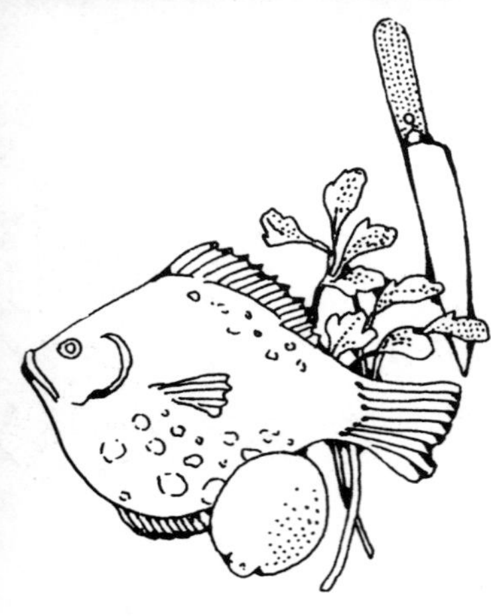

Red salmon	2 7 3/4-oz (220-g) cans
Onion	1 small, finely chopped
Eggs	2, lightly beaten
Whipping cream	1/2 cup (125 mL)
Brandy	1 1/2 Tbsp (20 mL)
Pepper	1/2 tsp (2 mL)
Sole fillets	10 large
White wine	1/3 cup (75 mL)
Lemons	2, sliced
Fresh parsley	12 sprigs, for garnish
Sauce	
Tomato	1, seeded and finely chopped
Red onion	1/3 cup (75 mL) chopped
Fresh parsley	3 Tbsp (50 mL) chopped
Capers	2 Tbsp (25 mL) chopped
Olive oil	6 Tbsp (100 mL)
Lemon juice	1/4 cup (50 mL)
Dried tarragon	1/4 tsp (1 mL)
Salt	1/2 tsp (2 mL)
Pepper	1/4 tsp (1 mL)

1 Drain salmon and remove any bone. Thaw sole fillets if necessary.

2 Combine salmon, onion, eggs, cream, brandy and pepper and mix until light and fluffy. Taste and add salt only if needed.

3 Pat fillets dry with paper towels. Spoon an equal amount of salmon mousse along narrow end of each fillet, then roll up. Place fillets seam side down in a greased ovenproof dish. Cover and refrigerate.

4 To make sauce combine ingredients in a jar and shake vigorously. Cover and store in refrigerator.

Last minute preparation Remove fillets and sauce from refrigerator and let stand at room temperature for 20 minutes. Add wine to bottom of casserole and bake, covered, at 350°F (180°C) for approximately 20 minutes. Test by inserting a fork into flesh and giving a slight twist. If fish breaks into flakes, it is cooked. To serve gently place fillets on a platter and garnish with parsley and lemon slices. Shake sauce well and serve separately.

NOODLES ALFREDO

Butter	3/4 cup (175 mL)
Light cream	3/4 cup (175 mL)
Parmesan cheese	1 1/3 cups (325 mL) grated
Fresh parsley	2 Tbsp (25 mL) chopped
Salt	3 1/2 tsp (17 mL)
Pepper	1/4 tsp (1 mL)
Oil	2 tsp (10 mL)
Egg noodles	12 oz (375 g)

1 In a small saucepan heat butter and cream over low heat, then stir in cheese, parsley, 1/2 tsp (2 mL) salt and pepper. Cover and store in refrigerator.

Last minute preparation Bring 4 quarts (4 L) water to a full boil. Add 3 tsp (15 mL) salt and oil. Stir in noodles and cook, uncovered, at full boil, stirring occasionally. Warm the sauce, but do not boil. When noodles are tender but firm, drain. Rinse with cold water, then hot water and drain again. Combine sauce and noodles, stirring until noodles are well coated. Keep warm.

ATLANTA GREEN BEANS

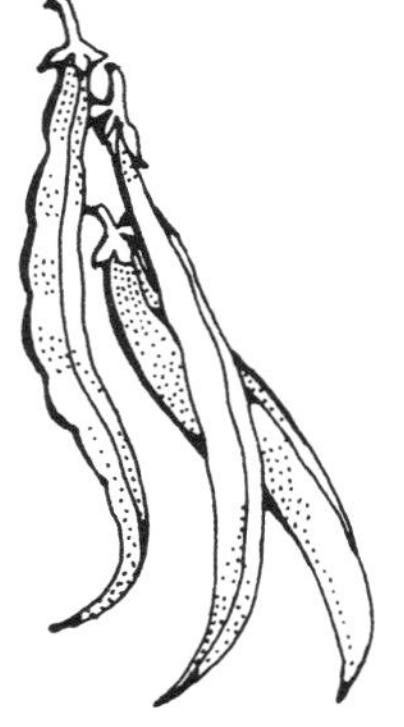

Fresh green beans	1 1/2 lbs (750 g)
Fresh button mushrooms	1/2 lb (250 g)
Butter	3 Tbsp (50 mL)
Slivered almonds	1/4 cup (50 mL)
Salt	3/4 tsp (4 mL)
Dried savory	1/4 tsp (1 mL)

1 Wash and trim green beans and cook in lightly salted water until just tender. Do not overcook. Drain and immerse in cold water to stop cooking process.

2 Clean mushrooms. Melt butter and sauté almonds and mushrooms until light brown.

3 Drain beans and combine with mushrooms, almonds, salt and savory. Put in ovenproof serving dish, cover and refrigerate.

Last minute preparation Reheat, covered, at 350°F (180°C) until hot, approximately 15 minutes.

SAUCY BEETS

Beets	3 lbs (1.5 kg)
Raisins	1 cup (250 mL)
Cornstarch	2 Tbsp (25 mL)
Sugar	1/2 cup (125 mL)
Salt	1 tsp (5 mL)
Pepper	1/4 tsp (1 mL)
Ground nutmeg	pinch
Orange juice	6 Tbsp (100 mL)
Butter	1/3 cup (75 mL)

1 Wash beets, cover with salted water and cook, covered, for about 1 hour until tender.

2 Drain under cold water, rub off skin and cut off tops and root end. Slice and store in covered container.

3 In a medium-sized saucepan heat 1 cup (250 mL) water and raisins over medium heat until raisins are plump.

4 Combine cornstarch, sugar, salt, pepper and nutmeg, then add orange juice and 1/2 cup (125 mL) water and mix well. Add to raisin mixture along with butter and beets and cook, stirring constantly until mixture boils and thickens. Cool, cover and refrigerate.

Last minute preparation Gently reheat beets and sauce on stove top until warm, about 10 minutes.

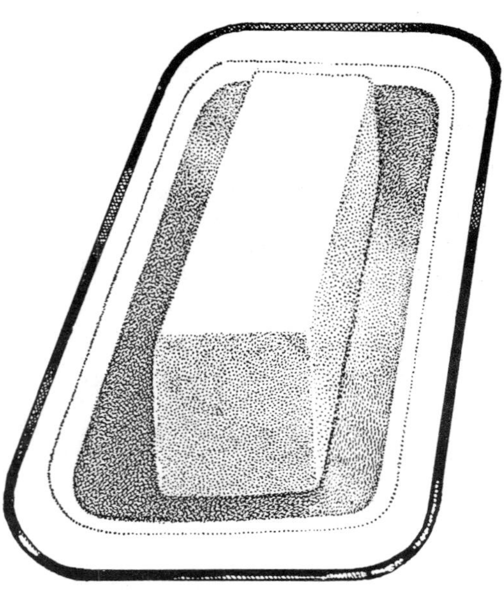

CHOCOLATE AMARETTO CHEESECAKE

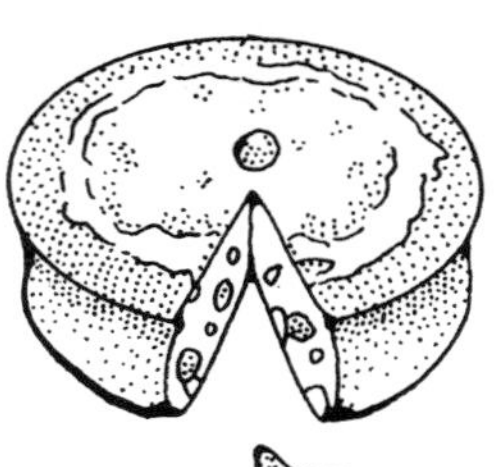

Chocolate wafer crumbs	1 cup (250 mL)
Ground almonds	1/2 cup (125 mL)
Sugar	2 Tbsp (25 mL)
Butter	1/4 cup (50 mL) melted
Semi-sweet chocolate	6 oz (175 g)
Cream cheese	16 oz (500 g)
Sugar	1/2 cup (125 mL)
Eggs	2
Almond extract	1/2 tsp (2 mL)
Amaretto liqueur	8 Tbsp (125 mL)
Sour cream	2/3 cup (150 mL)
Sliced almonds	1/3 cup (75 mL)
Whipping cream	1 cup (250 mL)

1 One day in advance, mix chocolate wafer crumbs, ground almonds, 2 Tbsp (25 mL) sugar and melted butter together and press into bottom and half way up the sides of a 9-inch (3-L) spring-form pan. Chill.

2 Melt chocolate over hot water and cool.

3 With an electric mixer, beat together cream cheese, sour cream and sugar until smooth. Add eggs, one at a time, beating well after each addition.

4 Add chocolate, almond extract and 6 Tbsp (100 mL) Amaretto liqueur and beat until blended. Pour into prepared crust and bake at 300°F (150°C) for 1 hour. Cool in oven with door ajar, then chill for 24 hours.

5 Toast almonds by baking at 350°F (180°C) until they are golden in colour, about 8 minutes.

6 Whip cream and remaining 2 Tbsp (25 mL) Amaretto until stiff. Spread on top of cheesecake and sprinkle with lightly toasted sliced almonds. Note: Do not whip cream too far in advance.

Last minute preparation Remove sides from pan and let cake warm on counter for 30 minutes. This sinfully rich dessert will certainly bring requests for seconds, especially from chocolate lovers.

TIME AND TEMPERATURE CHART

8:10	Broil	Stuffed Mushroom Caps
8:50	350°F (180°C)	Stuffed Fillets of Sole
8:50	Stove top	Noodles
8:55	350°F (180°C)	Green Beans
8:55	Stove top	Saucy Beets

Gourmet Menu #6

Hors d'oeuvres	Smoked Salmon Pâté
First Course	Crème du Barry
Main Course	Éstouffade de Boeuf
	Potatoes Romanoff
	Tomatoes Provençale
	Avocado and Grapefruit Salad
Dessert	Grasshopper Pie

Co-op Chart

Host/Hostess	Éstouffade de Boeuf
Couple A	Smoked Salmon Pâté, Potatoes Romanoff
Couple B	Crème du Barry, Tomatoes Provençale
Couple C	Avocado and Grapefruit Salad, Grasshopper Pie

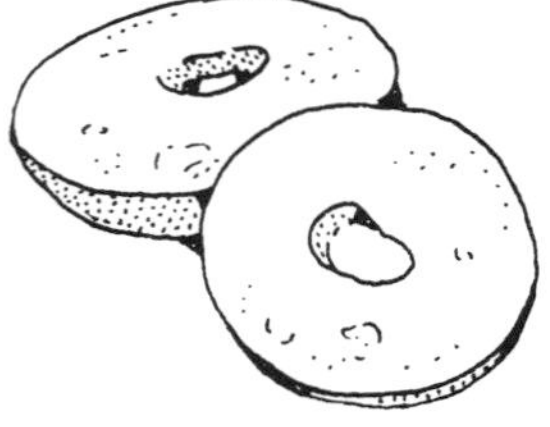

SMOKED SALMON PÂTÉ

Bagels	4
Pumpernickel bread	1 small loaf
Smoked salmon	6 oz (175 g)
Lemon juice	1 Tbsp (15 mL)
Lemon rind	1/2 tsp (2 mL) grated
Worcestershire sauce	1 tsp (5 mL)
Salt	1/2 tsp (2 mL)
Pepper	1/2 tsp (2 mL)
Cream cheese	8 oz (250 g)
Milk	2 Tbsp (25 mL)

1 Slice bagels across and cut into quarters. Cut pumpernickel bread into quarters. Store covered.

2 Chop salmon into small pieces. Combine with lemon juice and rind, Worcestershire sauce, salt and pepper.

3 In a food processor or blender process salmon mixture with cream cheese and milk until smooth and creamy. Put in an attractive serving dish, cover and refrigerate.

Last minute preparation Serve pâté surrounded by sliced bread and bagels.

CRÈME DU BARRY

Cauliflower	2 medium heads
Chicken stock	4 cups (1 L)
Butter	1/3 cup (75 mL)
Onion	1, chopped
Flour	2 Tbsp (25 mL)
Light cream	4 cups (1 L)
Salt	1 tsp (5 mL)
Pepper	1/2 tsp (2 mL)
Ground nutmeg	1/4 tsp (1 mL)
Fresh parsley	8 sprigs

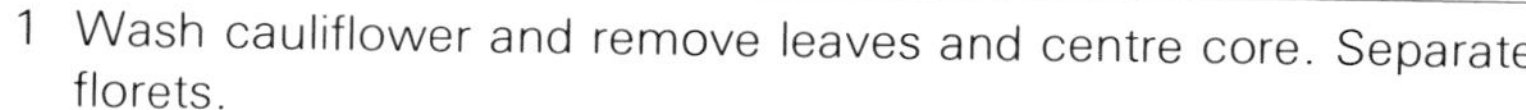

1 Wash cauliflower and remove leaves and centre core. Separate florets.

2 In a medium-sized pot bring chicken stock to a boil. Add cauliflower and cook until soft, 15 to 20 minutes. Remove cauliflower with slotted spoon, reserving stock. Purée cauliflower in blender or food processor or by hand.

3 In a large saucepan melt butter and sauté onion until transparent. Add flour and cook for 1 minute. Add reserved cooking stock and bring to a boil. Remove from heat. Add cauliflower purée, cream, salt, pepper and nutmeg. Cover, cool, and refrigerate.

Last minute preparation Heat soup, but do not boil. Serve in warm soup bowls and decorate with sprigs of parsley.

ÉSTOUFFADE DE BOEUF

Bacon drippings	8 Tbsp (125 mL)
Beef rump roast	4 1/2 lbs (2.2 kg)
Whole cloves	5
Onions	2, sliced
Carrots	2, peeled and quartered
Garlic	4 cloves
Cognac	1/2 cup (125 mL)
Dry red wine	1 cup (250 mL)
Bouquet garni	1 bag
Fresh parsley	1/4 cup (50 mL) chopped
Salt	1 tsp (5 mL)

1 In a Dutch oven melt bacon drippings over high heat. Add roast and brown on all sides.

2 Add remaining ingredients, cover and bake at 250°F (130°C) for 4 hours.

Last minute preparation Raise oven temperature to 300°F (150°C) and cook for 50 minutes. Remove meat to a carving platter, cover and let meat rest. After the first course strain pan juices into a gravy boat and slice meat.

POTATOES ROMANOFF

Potatoes	8 to 10 medium
Green onions	6, chopped
Salt	1 1/2 tsp (7 mL)
Pepper	1/2 tsp (2 mL)
Sour cream	2 cups (500 mL)
Sharp Cheddar cheese	2 cups (500 mL) grated
Butter	3 Tbsp (50 mL) melted

1 Peel and cut potatoes, then boil until tender. Drain well and mash.

2 Add onions, salt, pepper, sour cream and 1 1/2 cups (375 mL) cheese to the potatoes and mix well. Turn into a buttered dish, cover and refrigerate several hours.

Last minute preparation Brush top of potatoes with melted butter and bake, uncovered, at 300°F (150°C) for 40 minutes. Remove from oven, sprinkle with remaining cheese and return to oven for 20 minutes.

TOMATOES PROVENÇALE

Tomatoes	8 medium
Olive oil	6 Tbsp (100 mL)
Garlic	4 cloves, minced
Salt	1 tsp (5 mL)
Pepper	1 tsp (5 mL)
Fresh parsley	2 Tbsp (25 mL) chopped
Fresh basil	3 tsp (15 mL) chopped
Dried oregano	1 tsp (5 mL)
Dry bread crumbs	1/3 cup (75 mL)

1 Halve tomatoes crosswise and remove seeds by squeezing lightly. In a large frying pan, heat oil and garlic and place tomatoes cut-side down and cook over medium heat for 3 minutes.

2 Turn tomatoes over and transfer to an ovenproof dish.

3 In same frying pan heat salt, pepper, parsley, basil and oregano together. Pour over tomatoes. Cool, cover and refrigerate.

Last minute preparation Top tomatoes with bread crumbs. Broil for 5 minutes until golden brown on top.

AVOCADO AND GRAPEFRUIT SALAD

Iceberg lettuce	2 heads
Grapefruit	2
Sugar	1/2 cup (125 mL)
Salt	1 tsp (5 mL)
Celery salt	1 tsp (5 mL)
Dry mustard	1 tsp (5 mL)
Paprika	1 tsp (5 mL)
Onion	1 tsp (5 mL) grated
Salad oil	1 cup (250 mL)
White vinegar	1/4 cup (50 mL)
Ripe avocados	2

1 Wash lettuce and tear into bite-sized pieces. Wrap in paper towels and store in plastic bag in refrigerator.

2 Cover unpeeled grapefruit with boiling water and let stand for 5 minutes. Peel and section fruit, removing membrane. Cover and store.

3 Make dressing by mixing sugar, salt, celery salt, mustard, paprika and onion. Add oil, a small amount at a time, alternately with vinegar, the last addition being vinegar. Beat with a fork or shake in a jar. Store separately.

Last minute preparation Peel avocados, cut into cubes and toss with grapefruit to prevent discolouration. Mix lettuce, avocado and grapefruit and drizzle with dressing to coat. Serve immediately.

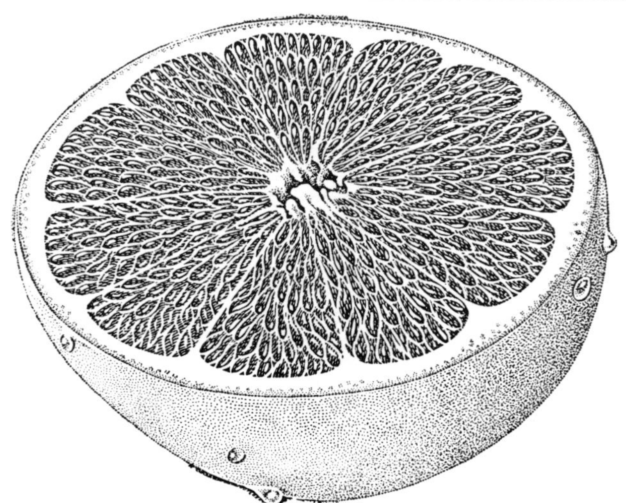

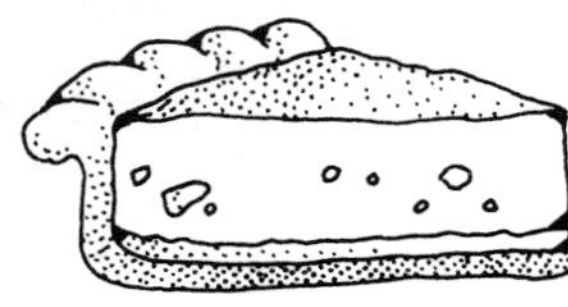

GRASSHOPPER PIE

Chocolate wafers	24, crushed
Butter	1/3 cup (75 mL) melted
Unflavoured gelatin	1 envelope
Water	1/2 cup (125 mL)
Egg yolks	3, at room temperature
Sugar	2/3 cup (150 mL)
Green crème de menthe	1/2 cup (125 mL)
Crème de cacao	1/3 cup (75 mL)
Egg whites	4, at room temperature
Salt	1/8 tsp (0.5 mL)
Whipping cream	1 cup (250 mL)
Semi-sweet chocolate	1 oz (30 g)

1 Combine wafer crumbs and butter, mix well and press into 9-inch (3-L) spring-form pan. Bake at 350°F (180°C) for 10 minutes, then cool

2 Sprinkle gelatin over cold water and let stand for 5 minutes. Add egg yolks and 1/3 cup (75 mL) sugar and mix well. Cook in top of double boiler until mixture thickens slightly, about 5 minutes. Remove from heat, add liqueurs and cool.

3 Beat egg whites with salt until soft peaks form. Gradually add remaining 1/3 cup (75 mL) sugar, beating until stiff peaks form. Gently fold gelatin mixture into egg whites.

4 Whip cream until stiff, then gently fold into liqueur mixture. Spoon into cooled crust and refrigerate at least 4 hours.

5 Decorate with chocolate curls made by running a knife or vegetable peeler over chocolate at room temperature.

Last minute preparation Serve this refreshing dessert well chilled.

TIME AND TEMPERATURE CHART

8:10	300°F (150°C)	Éstouffade de Boeuf Potatoes Romanoff
8:50	Stove top	Crème du Barry
9:10	Broil	Tomatoes Provençale

Gourmet Menu #7

Hors d'oeuvres	Caviar Mold Mushroom Pastries
Main Course	Coq au Vin Broccoli Soufflé Parsley Potatoes Tomatoes Vinaigrette
Dessert	Meringues with Apple Foam

Co-op Chart

Host/Hostess	Coq au Vin
Couple A	Caviar Mold, Parsley Potatoes
Couple B	Mushroom Pastries, Meringues with Apple Foam
Couple C	Tomatoes Vinaigrette, Broccoli Soufflé

CAVIAR MOLD

Unflavoured gelatin	1 envelope
Water	1/4 cup (50 mL)
Cream cheese	4 oz (125 g)
Caviar	1 2-oz (57-g) jar
Mayonnaise	3 Tbsp (50 mL)
Lemon juice	2 Tbsp (25 mL)
Tabasco sauce	2 drops
Onion	1 1/2 tsp (7 mL) grated
Unsalted crackers or Melba toast	assortment

1 In a small saucepan soak gelatin in water for 5 minutes, then heat over medium heat until dissolved.

2 With electric mixer beat cream cheese and add gelatin, caviar, mayonnaise, lemon juice, Tabasco and grated onion and mix well. Set aside until it begins to set.

3 Beat with electric mixer until fluffy. Turn into a small oiled mold. Cover and refrigerate.

Last minute preparation Turn mold onto platter and serve with plain, crisp crackers or Melba toast.

MUSHROOM PASTRIES

Cream cheese	8 oz (250 g), at room temperature
Butter	3/4 cup (175 mL)
All-purpose flour	1 1/2 cups (375 mL)
Fresh mushrooms	1/2 lb (250 g)
Green onions	2, chopped
Sherry	3 Tbsp (50 mL)
Ground nutmeg	1/4 tsp (1 mL)
Salt	1/2 tsp (2 mL)
Pepper	1/8 tsp (0.5 mL)
Flour	3 Tbsp (50 mL)
Sour cream	1/4 cup (50 mL)

1. Combine cream cheese and all but 3 Tbsp (50 mL) butter and mix until smooth. Work in 1 1/2 cups (375 mL) flour until well blended, then chill at least one hour.
2. In a skillet melt 3 Tbsp (50 mL) butter and sauté mushrooms and onions for 5 minutes.
3. Add sherry, nutmeg, salt, pepper and 3 Tbsp (50 mL) flour and stir well. Add sour cream and continue cooking gently until thick, then cool.
4. Roll dough to 1/8-inch (3-mm) thickness and cut into 2-inch (5-cm) circles.
5. Place 2 tsp (10 mL) of filling on each circle. Moisten edges lightly with water, then place a second circle on top. Press edges together firmly and prick tops carefully. Placed on ungreased cookie sheets and store, covered, in refrigerator.

Last minute preparation Bake, uncovered, at 375°F (190°C) for 15 minutes until golden and serve warm.

COQ AU VIN

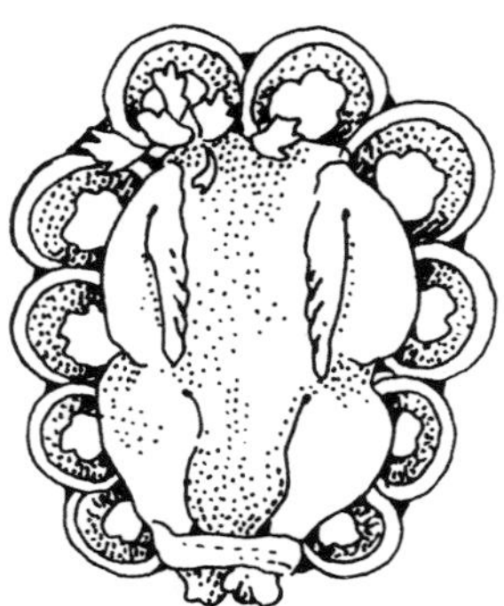

Bacon	1/2 lb (250 g)
Chicken breasts and/or legs	10 to 12 pieces
Salt	1 tsp (5 mL)
Pepper	1/4 tsp (1 mL)
Burgundy wine	3 cups (750 mL)
Garlic	2 cloves, minced
Dried thyme	1/2 tsp (2 mL)
Fresh parsley	1 tsp (5 mL) chopped
Small white onions	10, peeled and left whole
Fresh mushrooms	1 lb (500 g), cleaned and sliced
Butter	2 Tbsp (25 mL)
Cornstarch	2 Tbsp (25 mL)

1 Cut bacon into 1-inch (2.5-cm) pieces and fry in a heavy frying pan over medium heat. When lightly browned, remove bacon but leave the fat.

2 Brown chicken on all sides in hot bacon fat, cooking dark meat 10 minutes longer than white. Add salt, pepper, cooked bacon, red wine, garlic, thyme, parsley and onions. Cover and simmer for 50 minutes, or until chicken is tender. Remove from heat and cool.

3 Drain cooking liquid into a saucepan; cover and refrigerate chicken pieces.

4 Lightly sauté mushrooms in butter for 4 minutes. Add to chicken stored in refrigerator.

5 Skim fat from cooking liquid and bring to a boil. Combine cornstarch and 2 Tbsp (25 mL) water and add to cooking liquid, stirring until thickened. Remove from heat and cool.

6 Combine sauce, chicken, onions and mushrooms in a heavy covered saucepan. Refrigerate.

Last minute preparation Bring sauce to a gentle boil, reduce heat and simmer gently for 15 minutes, basting chicken if needed. With the meal serve the same burgundy wine as used in the cooking.

BROCCOLI SOUFFLÉ

Fresh broccoli	2 bunches, about 1 1/2 lbs (750 g)
Lemon juice	1 Tbsp (15 mL)
Butter	1/4 cup (50 mL)
Flour	1/4 cup (50 mL)
Milk	1 cup (250 mL)
Salt	1/2 tsp (2 mL)
Pepper	1/8 tsp (0.5 mL)
Ground nutmeg	1/8 tsp (0.5 mL)
Cayenne pepper	pinch
Eggs	4, separated
Parmesan cheese	1/2 cup (125 mL) grated

1 Wash broccoli, cut into pieces and cook in 1 inch (2.5 cm) boiling salted water with lemon juice. Cook for 5 to 8 minutes; should be slightly crisp and bright green. Drain well and purée in blender or food processor.

2 In a medium-sized saucepan melt butter and blend in flour until smooth. Gradually add milk, stirring constantly. Cook over medium heat, stirring until smooth and thickened.

3 Remove from heat and add salt, pepper, nutmeg, cayenne and egg yolks, one at a time. Stir in all but 2 Tbsp (25 mL) Parmesan cheese and broccoli purée. Cover and refrigerate.

4 Thoroughly butter a 6-cup (1 1/2-L) soufflé dish or straight sided ovenproof casserole and lightly dust with 2 Tbsp (25 mL) Parmesan cheese.

Last minute preparation Have broccoli mixture at room temperature. Beat egg whites until they form soft peaks. Add one quarter to broccoli mixture and combine well. Add remaining egg whites and gently fold in. Do not over mix. Turn into prepared dish and bake at 400 °F (200 °C) for 25 minutes. Do not open oven during baking period. Carry directly from oven to table and serve immediately; a soufflé waits for no one. Cut soufflé vertically to give everyone both crust and creamy interior.

PARSLEY POTATOES

Small new or red potatoes	3 lbs (1.5 kg)
Butter	1/4 cup (50 mL)
Fresh parsley	1/3 cup (75 mL) chopped

1 Wash potatoes. For a decorative touch remove a thin strip of skin from around the centre with a vegetable parer or sharp knife. Store covered with water.

Last minute preparation Gently boil potatoes in salted water for 25 minutes, or until tender. Drain. Toss with butter and fresh parsley. Serve hot.

TOMATOES VINAIGRETTE

Fresh parsley	1/4 cup (50 mL) chopped
Green onions	4, chopped
Firm, ripe tomatoes	6 to 8 medium
Salt	1/4 tsp (1 mL)
Pepper	1/4 tsp (1 mL)
Sugar	1/2 tsp (2 mL)
Wine vinegar	2 Tbsp (25 mL)
Dry mustard	1/4 tsp (1 mL)
Olive oil	6 Tbsp (100 mL)
Fresh basil	1 Tbsp (15 mL) chopped

1 Sprinkle half of chopped parsley and green onions on the bottom of a flat serving dish.

2 Cut out stem ends from tomatoes and slice. Arrange over chopped herbs and sprinkle with 1/8 tsp (0.5 mL) salt, pepper and sugar. Cover and refrigerate.

3 Make vinaigrette by shaking vinegar, 1/8 tsp (0.5 mL) salt, mustard and oil together in a jar.

4 If fresh basil is not available, chop together 1/2 tsp (2 mL) dried basil with 2 tsp (10 mL) chopped fresh parsley.

Last minute preparation Spoon enough vinaigrette over tomatoes to moisten. Top with remaining parsley, green onions and fresh basil. Cover and let stand for about 30 minutes. Serve at room temperature.

MERINGUES WITH APPLE FOAM

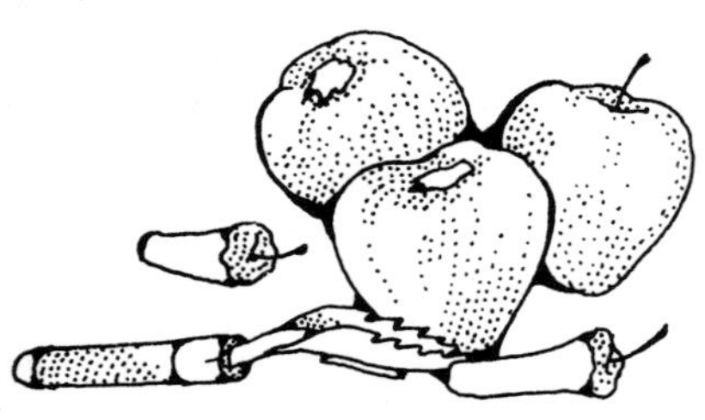

Egg whites	4
Vinegar	1 Tbsp (15 mL)
Water	1 Tbsp (15 mL)
Vanilla extract	1 tsp (5 mL)
Salt	1/4 tsp (1 mL)
Sugar	2 1/4 cups (550 mL)
Apples	4 large
Lemon juice	3 Tbsp (50 mL)
Whipping cream	1 1/2 cups (375 mL)
Brandy	2 Tbsp (25 mL)
Icing sugar	3 Tbsp (50 mL)

1 Preferably one day ahead, prepare the meringues. Beat egg whites until they are foaming, then add vinegar, water, vanilla and salt.

2 Slowly add 2 cups (500 mL) sugar, 2 Tbsp (25 mL) at a time, beating well between each addition. The mixture will be quite stiff when all the sugar has been incorporated.

3 Place paper towels on large baking sheets and mark 8 circles about 4 inches (10 cm) in diameter. Spoon meringue into nest shapes, forming the sides with the back of a spoon or use a pastry bag.

4 Place meringues in a preheated 325°F (160°C) oven and immediately turn off heat. With door closed, leave meringues in oven overnight. Store in an airtight container.

5 Peel, core and quarter apples. Slice each quarter into thin slices and sprinkle immediately with lemon juice and 1/4 cup (50 mL) sugar.

6 Whip cream with brandy and when almost stiff, add icing sugar. Refrigerate. Note: Do not whip cream too far in advance.

Last minute preparation At serving time fold apples into cream and spoon into meringue shells.

TIME AND TEMPERATURE CHART

8:10	375°F (190°C)	Mushroom Pastries
8:35	400°F (200°C)	Broccoli Soufflé
8:35	Stove top	Parsley Potatoes
8:45	Stove top	Coq au Vin

Gourmet Menu #8

Hors d'oeuvres	Cheese Clouds
	Sweet and Sour Sausage Balls
First Course	Chilled Tomato Consommé
Main Course	Paella
	Savory Broccoli
	Orange and Green Salad
Dessert	Mocha Coupes

Co-op Chart

Host/Hostess	Paella
Couple A	Cheese Clouds, Mocha Coupes
Couple B	Sausage Balls, Orange and Green Salad
Couple C	Chilled Consommé, Savory Broccoli

CHEESE CLOUDS

Unsliced sandwich bread	1 loaf
Cream cheese	4 oz (125 g)
Cheddar cheese	4 oz (125 g), grated
Butter	1/3 cup (75 mL)
White wine	2 Tbsp (25 mL)
Egg whites	2
Tabasco sauce	2 drops

1 Trim crusts from bread and cut into 1-inch (2.5-cm) slices. Cut into tiny circles with cookie cutter.

2 Melt cheese and butter over low heat, add wine and stir constantly until smooth.

3 Beat egg whites and Tabasco until stiff and gently fold into cheese mixture.

4 Dip bread into cheese mixture and coat well. Place on a greased cookie sheet, cover and refrigerate.

Last minute preparation Bake at 400°F (200°C) for 12 to 15 minutes, or until puffy and just turning brown. Serve hot.

SWEET AND SOUR SAUSAGE BALLS

Soft bread crumbs	1/3 cup (75 mL)
Bulk sausage meat	1 lb (500 g)
Dried thyme	1/2 tsp (2 mL)
Egg	1, lightly beaten
Fresh parsley	2 Tbsp (25 mL)
Ketchup	1 cup (250 mL)
Brown sugar	1/4 cup (50 mL)
Vinegar	3 Tbsp (50 mL)
Water	1/4 cup (50 mL)
Soy sauce	3 Tbsp (50 mL)
Green onions	2 Tbsp (25 mL) finely chopped

1 Combine bread crumbs with sausage meat, thyme, egg and parsley and shape into small balls.

2 Broil sausage balls in the oven or fry in a pan until golden all over. Drain well.

3 In a pot combine ketchup, brown sugar, vinegar, water, soy sauce and green onions. Simmer for 10 minutes. Add sausage balls and cook for 10 minutes. Refrigerate or freeze.

Last minute preparation Reheat in a pot on stove top until hot throughout, about 10 minutes, and serve with toothpicks. If sausage balls are frozen, thaw before reheating.

CHILLED TOMATO CONSOMMÉ

Unflavoured gelatin	2 envelopes
Tomato juice cocktail	2 cups (500 mL)
Condensed beef consommé soup	2 10-oz (284-mL) cans
Water	2 1/2 cups (625 mL)
Worcestershire sauce	2 tsp (10 mL)
Lemon juice	1 tsp (5 mL)
Whipping cream	1/4 cup (50 mL)
Lemon peel	1 tsp (5 mL) grated
Pimento	1 tsp (5 mL) chopped

1 Sprinkle gelatin over 1/2 cup (125 mL) tomato juice and set aside for 10 minutes.

2 In a large pot combine consommé, water, 1 1/2 cups (375 mL) tomato cocktail, Worcestershire sauce, lemon juice and gelatin mixture. Over medium heat, warm soup until gelatin dissolves. Remove from heat, cool and refrigerate.

3 Whip cream until thick and fold in lemon peel and pimento. Store covered. Note: Do not whip cream too far in advance of dinner.

Last minute preparation Serve soup in individual cups or bowls, topped with a spoonful of the whipped cream.

PAELLA

Fresh clams or mussels	24
Lean and boneless pork	1/2 lb (250 g)
Hot Italian sausage	1/2 lb (250 g)
Olive oil	3 Tbsp (50 mL)
Chicken thighs	10 small
Shelled raw shrimp	24 medium, deveined
Onions	3 large, chopped
Garlic	3 cloves, minced
Plum tomatoes	1 19-oz (540-mL) can, drained and chopped
Salt	1 1/2 tsp (7 mL)
Pepper	1/2 tsp (2 mL)
Chicken stock	5 cups (1.25 L)
Short grain rice	2 cups (500 mL)
Fresh green beans	1/2 lb (250 g), sliced
Saffron	pinch

1 Scrub clams or mussels well under cool running water to remove mud and encrustations. On mussels cut off the beard. Discard any cracked or broken shells. Put clams or mussels into a large pot of cold water with 2 Tbsp (25 mL) vinegar per quart (1 litre) of water and let clams or mussels sit for about 45 minutes. This will cause them to spit out any sand and grit. Rinse thoroughly and store in cold water until cooking time.

2 Cut pork into 3/4-inch (2-cm) pieces. Cut sausages into 1/2-inch (1.5-cm) pieces.

3 In a large frying pan or paella pan heat oil over medium heat. Add chicken and brown lightly on all sides, about 20 to 25 minutes. Remove from pan and set aside.

4 Add pork and sausages to the same pan and sauté until brown, 2 to 3 minutes. Remove and place with chicken.

5 Sauté shrimp in same pan for 1 to 2 minutes. Remove and store in a separate container.

Clockwise: Chilled Tomato Consommé (page 95); Orange and Green Salad (page 98); Paella (page 96).

6 Add 1 Tbsp (15 mL) oil to pan, if needed, and sauté onions and garlic until soft, about 5 to 8 minutes. Add tomatoes, salt and pepper and cook over medium heat until thick, about 10 minutes. Remove from heat and cool.

7 Combine tomato mixture with chicken, pork and sausage. Cover and refrigerate.

Last minute preparation Heat tomato and meat mixture over medium heat for 10 minutes. Add boiling stock, rice, green beans and saffron and bring to a boil. Transfer to a paella pan or a large shallow ovenproof casserole; you may have to use two casseroles. Lightly cover casserole with foil and bake at 375°F (190°C) for 15 minutes, then evenly distribute shrimp over the top of the rice and push down lightly. Add drained clams or mussels on top of the rice. Cover lightly again and return to oven and bake for 15 more minutes, or until rice is tender. Remove from oven and discard any clams or mussels that have not opened. Take pan or casserole to the table for serving.

SAVORY BROCCOLI

Fresh broccoli	2 bunches
Chicken stock	1 1/2 cups (375 mL)
Dried savory	1/2 tsp (2 mL)
Onions	2 medium, chopped
Lemon juice	1 Tbsp (15 mL)
Salt	1/2 tsp (2 mL)
Pepper	1/4 tsp (1 mL)
Butter	1/3 cup (75 mL)

1 Wash and trim broccoli and remove tough outer layer from stems. Slice stems and separate florets into small pieces. Store in plastic bag in refrigerator.

Last minute preparation In a large saucepan boil stock. Add broccoli, savory, onions, lemon juice, salt and pepper. Cover and simmer for 10 minutes, or until broccoli is tender. Drain, toss in butter and serve.

ORANGE AND GREEN SALAD

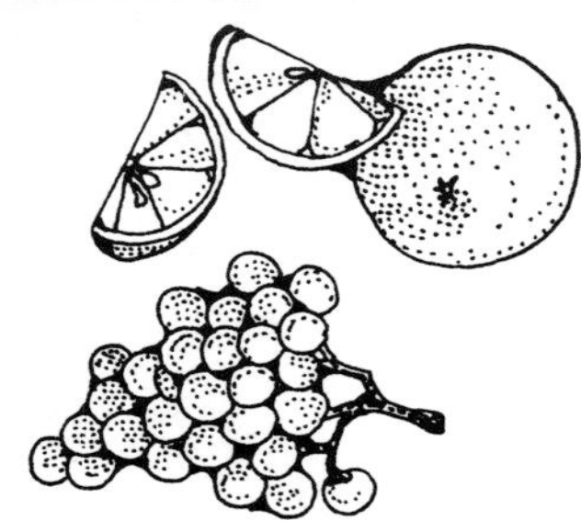

Boston lettuce	1 head
Iceberg lettuce	1 head
Oranges	4
Olive oil	1/3 cup (75 mL)
Red wine vinegar	6 tsp (30 mL)
Sugar	1/2 tsp (2 mL)
Salt	1/2 tsp (2 mL)
Pepper	1/4 tsp (1 mL)
Paprika	1/2 tsp (2 mL)
Red onion	1 medium, sliced in rings
Green seedless grapes	1/4 lb (125 g)

1 Wash lettuce and tear into bite-sized pieces. Wrap in paper towels and store in plastic bag in refrigerator.

2 Peel oranges, cut in half and slice thinly. Store separately.

3 Make dressing by combining oil, vinegar, sugar, salt, pepper and paprika and store in a jar.

Last minute preparation Combine lettuce, orange slices, onion rings and grapes. Shake dressing and add to salad, tossing to combine well.

MOCHA COUPES

Sliced almonds	1/2 cup (125 mL)
Whipping cream	1 1/4 cups (300 mL)
Cappuccino or mocha chocolate bar	6 oz (175 g)
Vanilla ice cream	1 quart (1 L)
Coffee ice cream	1 quart (1 L)
Coffee or chocolate liqueur	1/2 cup (125 mL)

1 Toast almonds in a 350°F (180°C) oven until golden brown. Store.

2 Whip 1 cup (250 mL) cream until stiff. Cover and refrigerate. Note: Do not whip cream too far in advance of dinner.

Last minute preparation After the main course, melt chocolate with 1/4 cup (50 mL) cream in a double boiler, stirring until smooth. Keep melted chocolate over warm water. Into each parfait glass or dish put a scoop of vanilla ice cream, a layer of chocolate sauce, then coffee ice cream. Add 1 Tbsp (15 mL) coffee liqueur and top with whipped cream and a sprinkling of almonds.

TIME AND TEMPERATURE CHART

8:05	400°F (200°C)	Cheese Clouds
8:10	Stove Top	Sausage Balls
8:30	Stove Top	Paella
8:40	375°F (190°C)	Paella
8:55	Stove Top	Savory Broccoli

International Menus

Chinese	First Course	Won Ton Soup
	Main Course	Beef and Broccoli Cashew Chicken Fish in Tomato Sauce Sweet and Sour Pork Shrimp with Vegetables Cucumber Salad Steamed Rice
	Dessert	Ginger Sherbet and Almond Cookies
French #1	Hors d'oeuvres	Hot Brie with Filberts
	First Course	Spinach Crêpe Cups
	Main Course	Duck Montmorency Duchess Potatoes Asparagus with Hollandaise Sauce Tomato and Cucumber Salad
	Dessert	Crème Caramel
French #2	Hors d'oeuvres	Crab and Bacon Rolls Roquefort Quiche Tarts
	Main Course	Veal Cordon Bleu Ratatouille Pommes Anna Green Salad with Garlic Dressing
	Dessert	Cherries Jubilee
German	Hors d'oeuvres	Brandied Pâté
	First Course	Hot Beer Soup
	Main Course	Beef Rouladen Dilled Carrot Coins Onion-Potato Pancakes Red Cabbage and Apple Salad
	Dessert	Black Forest Cake
Hawaiian	Hors d'oeuvres	Teriyaki Banana Appetizers Fish and Fruit Kebobs
	Main Course	Beef with Papaya Chicken with Ginger Green Beans Orientale Coconut Sweet Potatoes Curried Rice
	Dessert	Coconut-Pineapple Ice Cream and Fresh Fruit

Italian #1	First Course	Minestrone Soup
	Second Course	Fettucine with Spinach and Cheese
	Main Course	Chicken Cacciatore Stuffed Eggplant Italian Asparagus Romaine Salad
	Dessert	Spumone
Italian #2	Hors d'oeuvres	Prosciutto Sandwiches
	First Course	Tonnato
	Main Course	Veal Scallopine al Marsala Manicotti Florentine Mixed Vegetables
	Salad Course	Caesar Salad
	Dessert	Chilled Zabaglione Cream
Mexican	Hors d'oeuvres	Sangria and/or Margarita Cocktails Salsa Cruda and Tortilla Chips
	Main Course	Tacos with Sour Cream Chicken Mole Spanish Rice Corn with Cream Green Peas Mexican Style
	Dessert	Almendrado
Scandinavian	First Course	Herring Salad Swedish Meatballs in Mushroom Sauce
	Main Course	Fisherman's Loaf with Shrimp Sauce Baked Ham with Spiced Prunes Sweet and Sour Cabbage Potatoes with Anchovies Cucumber and Grape Salad
	Dessert	Lemon Delight and Cinnamon Crisps

Chinese Menu

First Course	Won Ton Soup
Main Course	Beef and Broccoli
	Cashew Chicken
	Fish in Tomato Sauce
	Sweet and Sour Pork
	Shrimp with Vegetables
	Cucumber Salad
	Steamed Rice
Dessert	Ginger Sherbet and Almond Cookies

Co-op Chart

Host/Hostess	Beef and Broccoli, Cashew Chicken, Steamed Rice
Couple A	Won Ton Soup, Fish in Tomato Sauce
Couple B	Sweet and Sour Pork, Cucumber Salad
Couple C	Shrimp with Vegetables, Sherbet and Almond Cookies

Note The Chinese usually serve one course at a time, each one a different challenge to the taste buds. We will serve all main dishes together. There are numerous dishes on this menu, but each recipe serves only a small portion, which allows you to taste each and take refills of your favourite ones.

WON TON SOUP

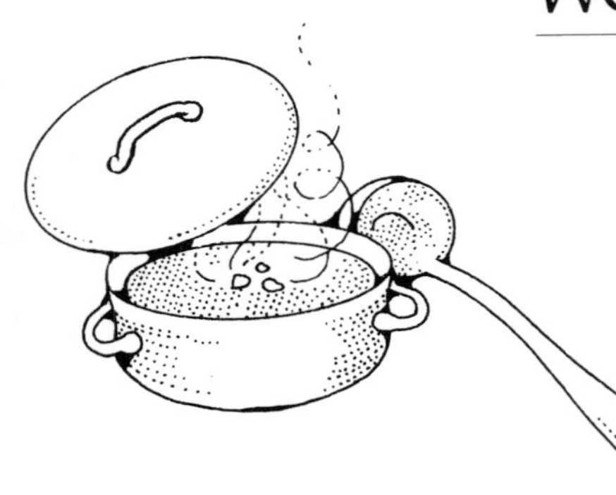

Ground pork	3/4 lb (375 g)
Egg	1 large
Green onions	1/3 cup (75 mL) chopped
Salt	2 tsp (10 mL)
Soy sauce	1/3 cup (75 mL)
Sesame or peanut oil	3 Tbsp (50 mL)
Won ton wrappers	1 package
Chicken stock	8 cups (2 L), fresh if possible
Carrot	1, peeled and shredded
Pepper	1/4 tsp (1 mL)
Cooked ham	1/3 cup (75 mL) shredded

1 Thaw wrappers if necessary.

2 To make filling combine pork, egg, 2 Tbsp (25 mL) green onion, 1 tsp (5 mL) salt, 2 Tbsp (25 mL) soy sauce and oil. Place 1 tsp (5 mL) filling in centre of each wrapper. Moisten edges with water and fold to make a triangle, then pinch together 2 outer corners to form a circle.

3 In a large pot bring 2 quarts (2 L) water to a boil. Add 1 tsp (5 mL) salt and 10 to 12 won tons. Cover and return to the boil.

4 Add 1/2 cup (125 mL) cold water and boil again. Remove won tons with a slotted spoon, drain and store covered. Repeat with remaining won tons.

5 To make the soup combine stock, carrot, remaining green onion, remaining soy sauce and pepper. Bring to a boil and simmer for 15 minutes. Cool and store, covered.

Last minute preparation Heat stock and add approximately 4 won tons per person and bring to a boil. Add finely shredded ham and serve in warm soup bowls.

BEEF AND BROCCOLI

Beef round steak	3/4 lb (375 g)
Sugar	1 tsp (5 mL)
Cornstarch	5 tsp (25 mL)
Soy sauce	3 tsp (15 mL)
Sherry	1 Tbsp (15 mL)
Fresh broccoli	6 cups (1 1/2 L), about 1 1/2 lbs (750 g)
Chicken stock	1 cup (250 mL)
Oyster sauce	2 Tbsp (25 mL)
Oil	4 tsp (20 mL)
Salt	1/2 tsp (2 mL)
Fresh ginger	1 piece, size of a quarter, grated

1 Slice beef across the grain in thin slices 3 inches (7 cm) long. Add sugar, 2 tsp (10 mL) cornstarch, 1 1/2 tsp (7 mL) soy sauce and sherry. Stir to combine and marinate for at least 30 minutes.

2 Wash broccoli and remove tough outer layer. Slice stems and divide florets into bite-sized pieces. Drop into boiling water for 30 seconds, then remove and rinse under cold running water. Set aside.

3 Combine stock, oyster sauce, remaining soy sauce and 3 tsp (15 mL) cornstarch.

Last minute preparation In a large frying pan or wok heat 4 tsp (20 mL) oil, salt and ginger for 1 minute. Add beef and stir-fry for one minute, then add broccoli and sauce mixture. Cook, stirring until gravy thickens. Serve hot.

CASHEW CHICKEN

Boned chicken breasts	4 single
Soy sauce	1/4 cup (50 mL)
Cornstarch	2 Tbsp (25 mL)
Cayenne pepper	1/8 tsp (0.5 mL)
Sugar	1/2 tsp (2 mL)
Salt	1/2 tsp (2 mL)
Oil	2 Tbsp (25 mL)
Green peppers	2, diced
Fresh mushrooms	1/2 lb (250 g), sliced
Water chestnuts	1 10-oz (284-mL) can, sliced
Green onions	10, chopped
Chicken stock	1 cup (250 mL)
Roasted cashew nuts	1/2 cup (125 mL)

1 Remove skin from chicken and slice in 1/2-inch (1-cm) thick slices.

2 Mix soy sauce, cornstarch, cayenne, sugar and salt and set aside.

3 In a wok or heavy frying pan heat oil and stir-fry chicken until meat turns white. Add green pepper, mushrooms, water chestnuts, green onions and stock and cook for 2 minutes.

4 Add soy sauce mixture and cook until sauce is thickened, stirring constantly. Remove from heat and put into a covered ovenproof casserole. Refrigerate.

Last minute preparation Reheat covered casserole at 325°F (160°C) for 20 minutes. Just before serving sprinkle with cashew nuts.

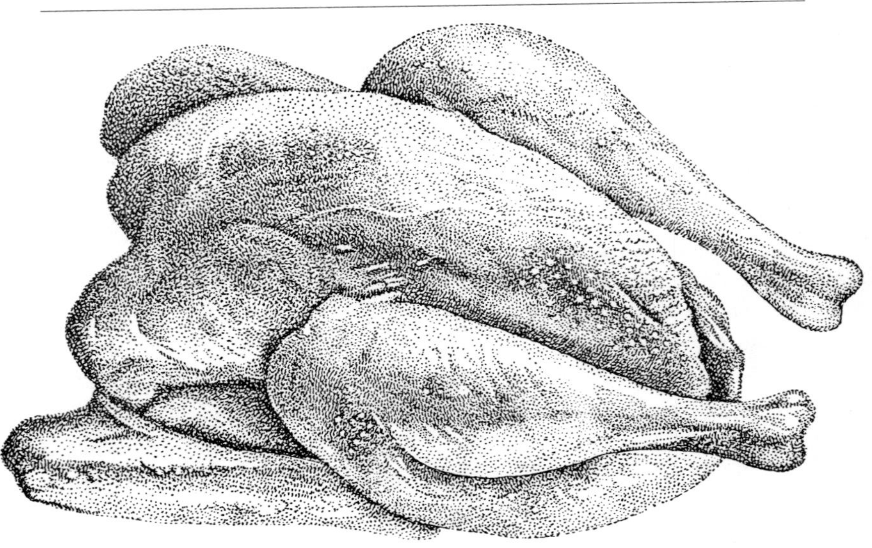

FISH WITH TOMATO SAUCE

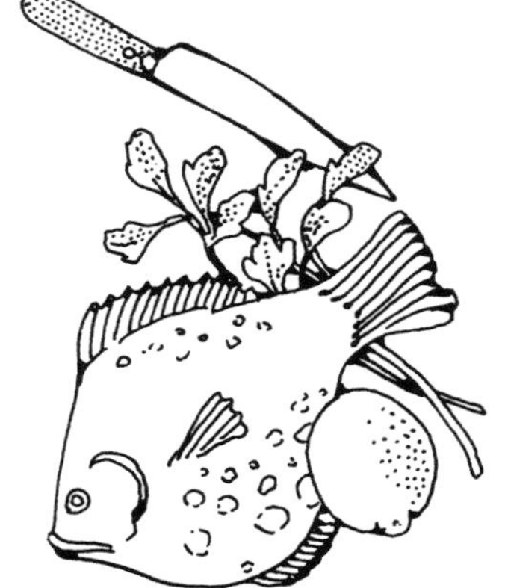

Dried Chinese mushrooms	5
Fillets of any white fish	1 lb (500 g)
Egg white	1
Cornstarch	3/4 cup (175 mL)
Salt	1 tsp (5 mL)
Sherry	2 tsp (10 mL)
Oil	2 cups (500 mL)
Onion	1/2 cup (125 mL) chopped
Carrot	1, julienned
Sugar	3 Tbsp (50 mL)
Vinegar	3 Tbsp (50 mL)
Water	6 Tbsp (100 mL)
Ketchup	3 Tbsp (50 mL)
Fresh or frozen green peas	1/4 cup (50 mL)

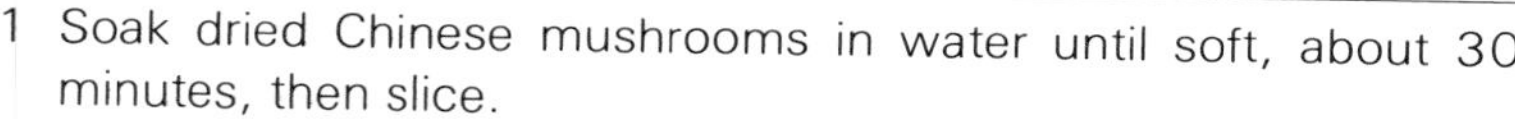

1 Soak dried Chinese mushrooms in water until soft, about 30 minutes, then slice.

2 Remove bones and skin from fish and cut into 1/2-inch (1-cm) thick slices, then into 2-inch (5-cm) squares.

3 Combine egg white, 1 Tbsp (15 mL) cornstarch, 1/2 tsp (2 mL) salt and sherry. Mix with fish pieces and let sit for one hour.

4 Heat 2 Tbsp (25 mL) oil in a frying pan and sauté onions, mushrooms and carrots until onions are transparent. Add sugar, vinegar, water, ketchup, 2 Tbsp (25 mL) cornstarch, 1/2 tsp (2 mL) salt and green peas, stirring until thick. Remove from heat and cool.

5 Heat remaining oil in a deep pot. Dip fish in remaining cornstarch, then fry until golden brown and drain well. Repeat until all fish is cooked. Refrigerate.

Last minute preparation Heat sauce on stove top or in oven. Warm fish in the oven, uncovered, 5 to 10 minutes. At the last minute put fish in a serving dish and cover with sauce. Stir gently to combine.

SWEET AND SOUR PORK

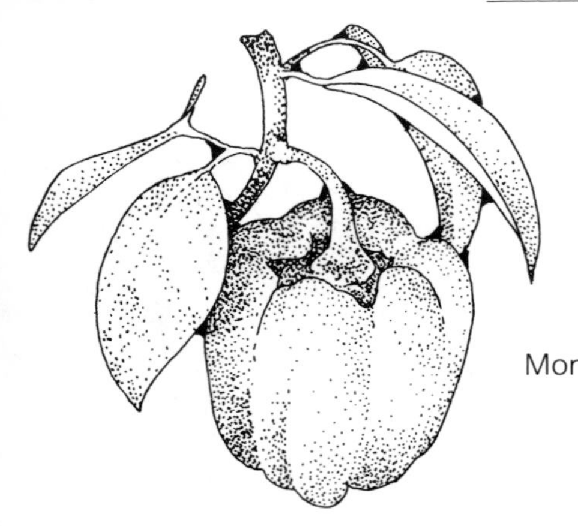

Pork tenderloin	1 lb (500 g)
Eggs	2
Flour	1/2 cup (125 mL)
Beer	3 Tbsp (50 mL)
Oil	2 cups (500 mL)
Vinegar	1/2 cup (125 mL)
Pepper	1/4 tsp (1 mL)
Soy sauce	4 tsp (20 mL)
Brown sugar	1/2 cup (125 mL)
Monosodium glutamate (MSG)	1 tsp (5 mL), optional
Garlic	3 cloves, minced
Salt	1 tsp (5 mL)
Cornstarch	2 Tbsp (25 mL)
Green peppers	2, seeded and cubed
Unsweetened pineapple chunks	1 14-oz (398-mL) can, drained and juice reserved

1 Cut pork into 1-inch (2.5-cm) squares, then dip in batter made by combining eggs, flour and beer.

2 Heat oil to 375°F (190°C) and cook a few pork cubes at a time until golden brown. Drain well. Repeat with remaining pork. Cover and refrigerate.

3 In a heavy pan combine vinegar, 1 cup (250 mL) pineapple juice, pepper, soy sauce, brown sugar, MSG, garlic and salt to make sweet and sour sauce and bring to a boil. Combine cornstarch and 2 Tbsp (25 mL) water and add to sauce, stirring until thickened. Add green peppers and pineapple. Remove from heat and store, covered, in refrigerator.

Last minute preparation Heat pork in 325°F (160°C) oven for 10 minutes. At the same time heat sauce on stove top over medium heat. Add pork and stir quickly but thoroughly until sauce coats all ingredients. Adding pork at last minute preserves the crispy coating on the pork cubes.

SHRIMP WITH VEGETABLES

Shelled raw shrimp	3/4 lb (375 g)
Dried Chinese mushrooms or large fresh mushrooms	8
Cornstarch	1 Tbsp (15 mL)
Sherry	1 Tbsp (15 mL)
Sugar	1/2 tsp (2 mL)
Soy sauce	2 tsp (10 mL)
Monosodium glutamate (MSG)	1/2 tsp (2 mL), optional
Oil	3 Tbsp (50 mL)
Chinese cabbage (bok choy)	1 1/2 cups (375 mL) sliced
Water chestnuts	15, sliced
Celery	4 ribs, sliced diagonally
Small button mushrooms	1/2 cup (125 mL)
Green beans	1/2 cup (125 mL) sliced
Chinese baby corn cobs	1 can, drained
Chicken stock	1/2 cup (125 mL)
Snow peas	20, washed and trimmed

1. Wash and clean shrimp. Boil just until the flesh turns pink, about 1 1/2 minutes. Rinse and chop coarsely.
2. Soak dried Chinese mushrooms for 30 minutes, or until soft, then slice.
3. Mix cornstarch, sherry, sugar, soy sauce and MSG and store separately.

Last minute preparation In a large frying pan or wok over high heat add oil, then add Chinese mushrooms, cabbage, water chestnuts, celery, mushrooms, green beans and corn cobs and stir-fry for 30 seconds. Add stock and cook for 2 minutes. Next add snow peas, shrimp and cornstarch solution and stir until sauce is thickened. Serve immediately.

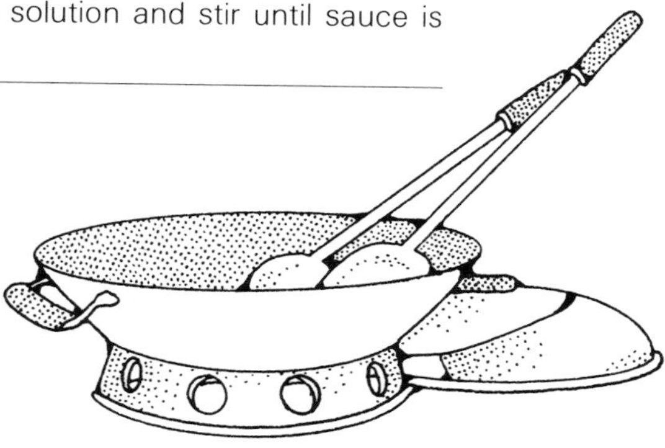

CUCUMBER SALAD

Cucumbers	2
Fresh or frozen shelled shrimp	1/2 lb (250 g)
White vinegar	1 cup (250 mL)
Fresh ginger	1 tsp (5 mL) finely grated
Sugar	4 tsp (20 mL)
Salt	1/4 tsp (1 mL)
Sesame seeds	2 Tbsp (25 mL)

1 Peel cucumber and thinly slice. Press out all liquid.

2 Clean and cook shrimp and halve each lengthwise.

3 Mix vinegar, ginger, sugar and salt together.

4 Toast sesame seeds and store separately.

Last minute preparation Pour vinegar mixture over cucumber and add shrimp. Sprinkle with sesame seeds and serve cold.

STEAMED RICE

Long grain rice	2 1/2 cups (625 mL)
Salt	1 1/2 tsp (7 mL)
Water	3 1/2 cups (875 mL)

1 Run cold water over rice in a sieve until water runs clear. Let drain and dry.

Last minute preparation Put rice in a large pot and add salt and water. Cover pot and place over high heat. When water boils, uncover pot and wait until nearly all the water is boiled away and the rice is visible under the mass of bubbles. Cover pot and turn to lowest heat. Steam for 15 minutes without removing lid. Fluff with a fork and serve.

GINGER SHERBET AND ALMOND COOKIES

Preserved ginger	1/3 cup (75 mL)
All-purpose flour	1 1/2 cups (375 mL)
Baking powder	1/2 tsp (2 mL)
Salt	1/8 tsp (0.5 mL)
Egg	1
Shortening	1/2 cup (125 mL)
Sugar	3/4 cup (175 mL)
Vanilla extract	1/4 tsp (1 mL)
Almond extract	1/4 tsp (1 mL)
Blanched almonds	20 to 24
Lemon or lime sherbet	1 quart (1 L)

1 Grate or finely chop ginger and store in a container.

2 Sift together flour, baking powder and salt.

3 Lightly beat egg and divide into two portions.

4 With an electric mixer cream shortening and sugar. Add one portion of egg, vanilla and almond extracts and mix. Add dry ingredients and mix.

5 Knead dough until firm. Roll into balls and flatten on a greased cookie sheet. Brush lightly with remaining beaten egg and decorate with blanched almonds. Bake at 350°F (180°C) for 10 to 15 minutes, or until lightly brown. Store, covered.

Last minute preparation Scoop sherbet into individual dishes and top with a sprinkling of preserved ginger. Serve with almond cookies.

TIME AND TEMPERATURE CHART

8:50	325°F (160°C)	Cashew Chicken Tomato sauce Sweet and Sour sauce
8:50	Stove top	Soup Rice
8:55	Stove top	Beef and Broccoli Shrimp with Vegetables
9:00	325°F (160°C)	Fish Pork cubes

French Menu #1

Hors d'oeuvres	Hot Brie with Filberts
First Course	Spinach Crêpe Cups
Main Course	Duck Montmorency
	Duchess Potatoes
	Asparagus with Hollandaise Sauce
	Tomato and Cucumber Salad
Dessert	Crème Caramel

Co-op Chart

Host/Hostess	Duck Montmorency
Couple A	Hot Brie with Filberts, Crème Caramel
Couple B	Spinach Crêpe Cups, Tomato and Cucumber Salad
Couple C	Duchess Potatoes, Asparagus with Hollandaise Sauce

HOT BRIE WITH FILBERTS

Brie cheese	8 oz (250 g)
Butter	3 Tbsp (50 mL)
Sliced filberts (hazelnuts)	1/3 cup (75 mL)
Crackers	assortment

Last minute preparation Place cheese on an ovenproof serving plate. In a small pan melt butter and sauté filberts until light brown. Spoon nuts and butter over cheese and bake at 350°F (180°C) for 12 to 15 minutes. Serve immediately with crackers.

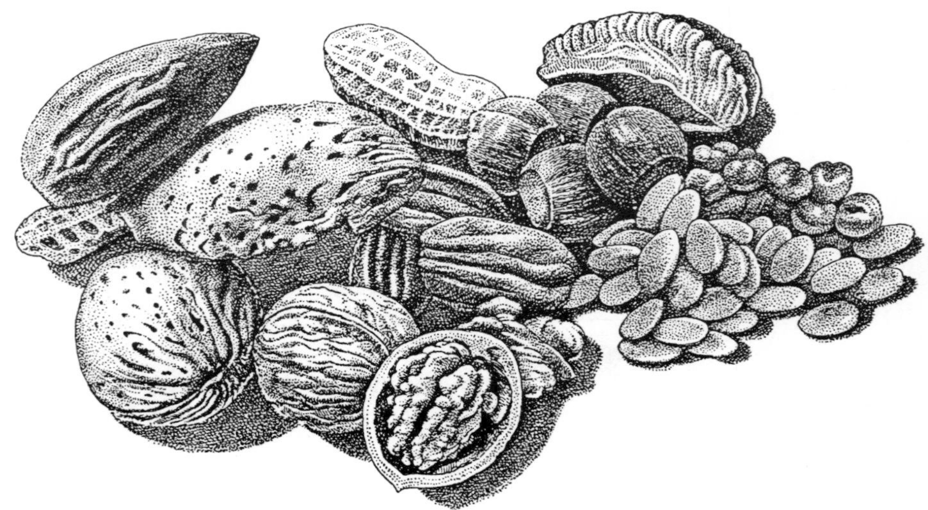

SPINACH CRÊPE CUPS

Eggs	6
All-purpose flour	2/3 cup (150 mL)
Salt	1 tsp (5 mL)
Milk	1 cup (250 mL)
Fresh spinach	10 oz (280 g)
Fresh mushrooms	10 medium, chopped
Green onions	2, chopped
Butter	2 Tbsp (25 mL)
Swiss cheese	1 1/2 cups (375 mL) shredded
Flour	3 Tbsp (50 mL)
Sour cream	3/4 cup (175 mL)
Cooked ham	1/3 cup (75 mL) finely chopped
Pepper	1/4 tsp (1 mL)

1. Beat 3 eggs, add 2/3 cup (150 mL) flour, 1/2 tsp (2 mL) salt and milk and continue beating until smooth. Refrigerate for one hour.
2. Lightly grease a 6-inch (15-cm) crêpe pan or small skillet and heat over medium-high heat. Add 2 Tbsp (25 mL) batter and cook until very lightly browned, then turn and brown other side.
3. Remove crêpe and let cool on clean surface. Repeat with remaining batter. Stack cooled crêpes between layers of waxed paper, cover with plastic wrap and refrigerate or freeze.
4. Wash spinach and cook in 1 Tbsp (15 mL) water until wilted. Drain well and chop. Sauté with mushrooms and green onions in butter for 4 minutes.
5. Mix cheese with 3 Tbsp (50 mL) flour. Add remaining 3 eggs, sour cream, spinach, onions, mushrooms, ham, 1/2 tsp (2 mL) salt and pepper and mix well. Cover and refrigerate.

Last minute preparation If crêpes are frozen, thaw first. Fit crêpes into greased muffin tins and add cheese mixture. Bake at 350°F (180°C) for 30 minutes, or until hot. Remove from baking tins and serve two crêpes per person.

DUCK MONTMORENCY

Ducks	2 6-lb (3-kg) birds
Salt	1 1/2 tsp (7 mL)
Pepper	1 tsp (5 mL)
Celery	2 ribs, cut in half
Orange	1, cut in half
Chicken stock	2 1/4 cups (550 mL)
Orange juice	1/4 cup (50 mL)
Port	3/4 cup (175 mL)
Cherry brandy	3/4 cup (175 mL)
Cornstarch	4 Tbsp (65 mL)
Pitted sour red cherries	2 14-oz (398-mL) cans, drained
Ground nutmeg	1/2 tsp (2 mL)

1 Wash ducks and dry thoroughly. Sprinkle salt and pepper and add celery and orange to each cavity. Roast on a rack, breast side up for 15 minutes at 450°F (230°C). Reduce heat to 350°F (180°C) and continue to roast until tender, about 18 minutes per pound, 40 minutes per kilogram. Turn ducks over once or twice to brown evenly.

Last minute preparation Remove ducks to warm platter. Skim off fat from liquid in roasting pan, leaving brown juice and sediment. Put pan over medium-high heat and add chicken stock and orange juice, scraping up all the browned bits. Reduce heat to medium and add port and brandy. Combine cornstarch and 1/2 cup (125 mL) canned cherry juice and slowly add one half to the pan, stirring constantly. Add remainder as required, until sauce reaches desired consistency. Add cherries and nutmeg and heat thoroughly. Using poultry shears, cut each duck in half lengthwise through the breast and along the back bone, then cut crosswise just under the ribs to make 4 servings per duck. Arrange pieces on a platter and pour sauce over top.

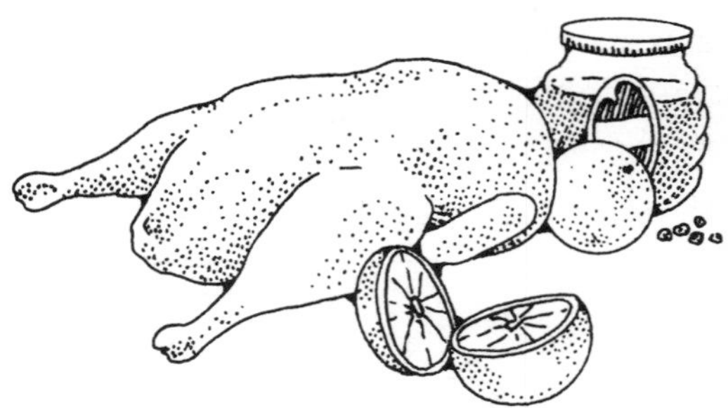

DUCHESS POTATOES

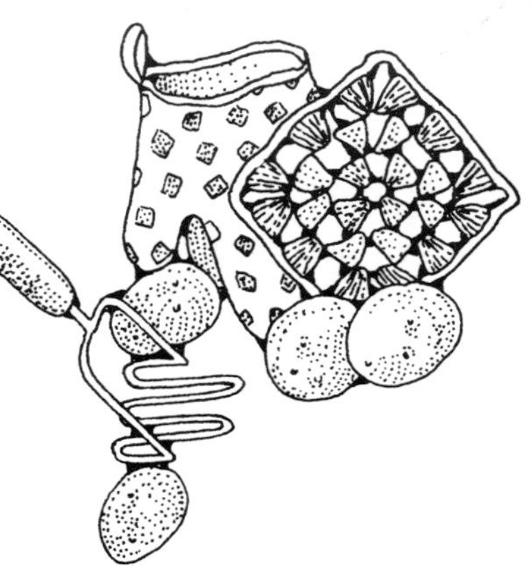

Potatoes	3 lbs (1.5 kg)
Butter	3/4 cup (175 mL) melted
Egg yolks	3, beaten
Salt	1/2 tsp (2 mL)
Pepper	1/4 tsp (1 mL)
Milk	1/4 cup (50 mL), approximately

1 Peel and cook potatoes, then drain and mash well. Add 1/2 cup (125 mL) melted butter, egg yolks, salt and pepper and beat with electric mixer until smooth. Add only enough milk to make mixture smooth and fluffy.

2 Using a pastry bag make 8 or 10 potato mounds on a lightly greased cookie sheet. Spoon remaining 1/4 cup (50 mL) melted butter over mounds and store well covered. The potatoes can also be placed in a buttered casserole with melted butter poured over top.

Last minute preparation Bake individual servings, uncovered, at 350°F (180°C) until brown and hot throughout, about 20 minutes. Casserole should be baked, uncovered, for 40 minutes.

ASPARAGUS WITH HOLLANDAISE SAUCE

Fresh asparagus	3 lbs (1.5 kg)
Egg yolks	3
Salt	1/2 tsp (2 mL)
Cayenne pepper	pinch
Fresh lemon juice	4 tsp (20 mL)
Butter	3/4 cup (175 mL) melted

1 Wash asparagus and break off tough ends. Store, covered, in refrigerator.

2 In a small container whisk egg yolks together with salt, cayenne and lemon juice. Cover and refrigerate.

Last minute preparation Place asparagus in steamer basket and steam over boiling water until just tender, about 10 minutes. Meanwhile, prepare sauce in a double boiler. Over medium-low heat, add egg yolk mixture and slowly drip in melted butter, stirring constantly until sauce is smooth and slightly thickened. Remove from heat and set in a bowl of warm water, stirring occasionally. Do not let sauce get too hot or you will have scrambled eggs.

Alternate method: In a blender put egg yolks, salt, cayenne and lemon juice and process for 1 minute until frothy. Slowly dribble in melted butter, keeping blender on medium speed until thickened. Set in a bowl of warm water until serving time. To serve, pour warm hollandaise sauce over asparagus.

TOMATO AND CUCUMBER SALAD

Tomatoes	6
Cucumber	1 large
Vegetable oil	6 Tbsp (100 mL)
Vinegar	2 Tbsp (25 mL)
Salt	1 tsp (5 mL)
Pepper	1/4 tsp (1 mL)
Sugar	3/4 tsp (3 mL)
Fresh parsley	3 Tbsp (50 mL) minced
Green onions	3, minced

1 Peel and core tomatoes and slice thinly. Peel and thinly slice cucumber. Refrigerate separately.

2 Make dressing by combining oil, vinegar, salt, pepper, sugar, parsley and green onions. Store in a jar.

Last minute preparation Arrange tomatoes and cucumber slices on a shallow platter and drizzle with dressing. Serve at room temperature.

CRÈME CARAMEL

Sugar	1 1/3 cups (300 mL)
Water	1/3 cup (75 mL)
Milk	4 cups (1 L)
Pure vanilla extract	2 tsp (10 mL)
Eggs	6
Egg yolks	6

1 In a small saucepan combine 2/3 cup (150 mL) sugar and water. Bring syrup to a boil and carefully continue to heat until it becomes a rich caramel brown. As the syrup darkens, the flavour improves, but care must be taken to prevent burning.

2 Pour caramel into a 6 to 8-cup (1 1/2 to 2-L) metal mold (such as a charlotte pan) or 8 individual custard cups. Tip the pan or cups to coat the bottom and halfway up the sides with caramel. When the caramel stops running (in about 4 minutes), turn the mold or cups upside down over a plate and cool.

3 Heat milk to just below boiling and remove from heat and add vanilla extract. Set aside for a few minutes.

4 In a large bowl beat eggs and yolks with an electric mixer and gradually add 2/3 cup (150 mL) sugar until light and foamy. Gradually add hot milk in a slow stream while continuing to beat. Strain mixture into caramel-lined mold or custard cups.

5 Place mold or custard cups in a baking pan and add enough water to immerse halfway. Bake at 325°F (160°C) for about 60 minutes, or until a knife inserted in the middle comes out clean. Cooking time for small cups will be about 40 minutes.

6 Remove from pan of water and cool. Cover and chill in refrigerator for at least 8 hours.

Last minute preparation Loosen the custard by running a knife or spatula around the edge. Place serving plate on top of mold and invert. If using custard cups, invert onto individual plates. Serve this classic French dessert cold.

TIME AND TEMPERATURE CHART

7:25	450°F (230°C)	Duck (time is approximate)
7:40	350°F (180°C)	Reduce temperature
8:10	355°F (180°C)	Hot Brie with Filberts
8:30	350°F (180°C)	Spinach Crêpe Cups
8:50	350°F (180°C)	Individual Duchess Potatoes
8:50	Stove top	Asparagus
		Hollandaise sauce

French Menu #2

Hors d'oeuvres	Crab and Bacon Rolls
	Roquefort Quiche Tarts
Main Course	Veal Cordon Bleu
	Ratatouille
	Pommes Anna
	Green Salad with Garlic Dressing
Dessert	Cherries Jubilee

Co-op Chart

Host/Hostess	Veal Cordon Bleu
Couple A	Crab and Bacon Rolls, Green Salad
Couple B	Quiche Tarts, Ratatouille
Couple C	Pommes Anna, Cherries Jubilee

CRAB AND BACON ROLLS

Crab meat	1 6-oz (170-g) can
Fresh bread crumbs	1/2 cup (125 mL)
Powdered ginger	1/2 tsp (2 mL)
Onion	1 Tbsp (15 mL) minced
Fresh parsley	1 Tbsp (15 mL) chopped
White wine	2 tsp (10 mL)
Egg	1
Salt	1/4 tsp (1 mL)
Tabasco sauce	dash
Pepper	pinch
Bacon	12 slices

1 Drain crab meat and remove cartilage. Combine with bread crumbs, ginger, onion, parsley, wine, egg, salt, Tabasco and pepper. Form into 24 balls.

2 Cut bacon strips in half and wrap one around each crab ball. Secure with a toothpick. Cover and refrigerate.

Last minute preparation Broil, turning frequently, until bacon is crisp.

ROQUEFORT QUICHE TARTS

Roquefort or blue cheese	3/4 cup (175 mL), at room temperature
Yogurt	1 1/4 cups (300 mL)
Eggs	3
Salt	1/4 tsp (1 mL)
Pepper	1/4 tsp (1 mL)
Nutmeg	pinch
Chives	1 tsp (5 mL) chopped
Baked tart shells	24 small
Butter	2 Tbsp (25 mL) melted

1 Mix Roquefort cheese until smooth, then add 1/2 cup (125 mL) of yogurt and combine well.

2 In a bowl beat eggs and add yogurt-cheese mixture, salt, pepper, nutmeg, chives and remaining yogurt. Combine well.

3 Pour into baked tart shells. Top each with a small dot of butter and bake at 350°F (180°C) for 20 to 25 minutes, until just lightly browned.

4 Remove from oven and cool. Cover and refrigerate.

Last minute preparation Reheat tarts at 350°F (180°C) for 5 to 8 minutes until hot. Let cool 5 minutes before removing from pans.

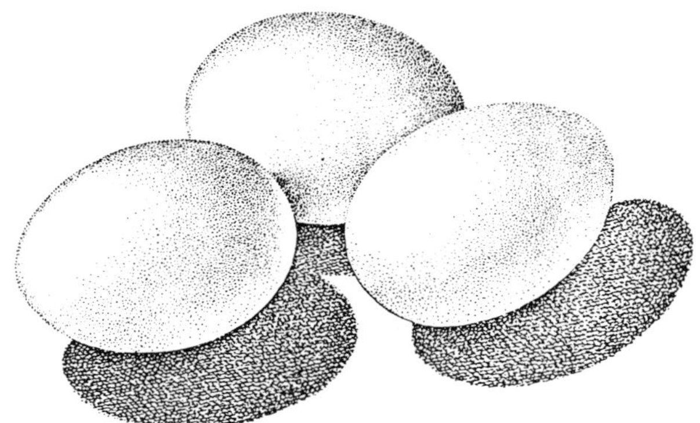

VEAL CORDON BLEU

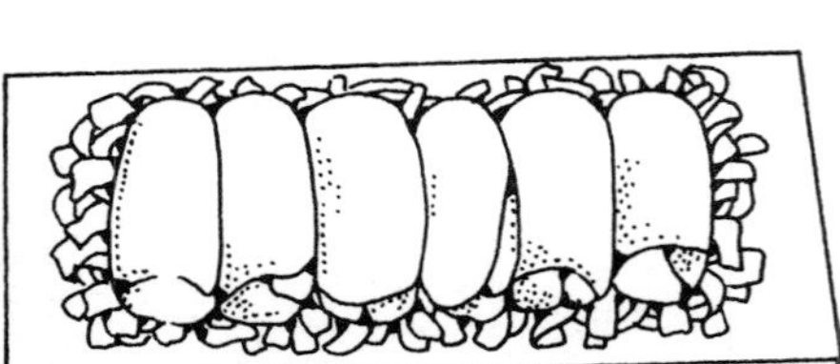

Boneless veal cutlets	10 4-oz (125 g) pieces, 1/2 inch (1 cm) thick
Prosciutto or ham	10 thin slices
Swiss cheese	10 slices
Eggs	2
Flour	6 Tbsp (100 mL)
Salt	1 tsp (5 mL)
Pepper	1/2 tsp (2 mL)
Paprika	1/2 tsp (2 mL)
Ground allspice	1/2 tsp (2 mL)
Dry bread crumbs	1 1/4 cups (300 mL)
Shortening	1/3 cup (75 mL)

1 Pound veal until very thin, being careful not to tear meat.

2 Place a slice of prosciutto on each piece of veal and top with a slice of cheese. Trim prosciutto and cheese to make them smaller than the veal.

3 Fold the two long sides of the veal over the cheese and ham. From the narrow end roll veal, jelly-roll style, keeping cheese sealed inside. Secure with toothpicks.

4 In a bowl beat eggs until fluffy. Combine flour, salt, pepper, paprika and allspice in another bowl. Pour bread crumbs into a third bowl.

5 Dredge each veal roll in flour, dip into eggs and then into bread crumbs. Pat gently to help crumbs adhere. Cover and refrigerate for at least one hour.

6 In a heavy skillet melt shortening and evenly brown veal rolls (a few at a time) about 5 minutes. Transfer to an ovenproof casserole. Cover and refrigerate.

Last minute preparation Bake covered casserole at 350°F (180°C) for 35 minutes. Uncover and continue baking for 10 minutes.

RATATOUILLE

Eggplant	1 large
Zucchini	1/2 lb (250 g)
Salt	1 tsp (5 mL)
Olive oil	4 to 5 Tbsp (65 to 85 mL)
Garlic	2 cloves, minced
Onions	4 medium, sliced
Ripe tomatoes	1 lb (500 g), peeled, coarsely chopped
Green pepper	1, seeded and diced
Sweet red pepper	1, seeded and diced
Fresh parsley	2 Tbsp (25 mL) chopped

1 Dice eggplant and slice zucchini, but do not peel either vegetable. Place in a colander, sprinkle lightly with salt and let sit for 30 minutes. This helps reduce bitter taste of eggplant and draws water from zucchini. Rinse and drain.

2 In a large pan heat olive oil and sauté garlic and onions for 5 minutes. Add tomatoes and cook gently for 3 to 4 minutes, then add all remaining ingredients and stir well. Remove from heat and transfer to ovenproof casserole. Cool and refrigerate.

Last minute preparation Bake, covered, at 350°F (180°C) for 30 minutes. Vegetables should retain individual textures.

POMMES ANNA

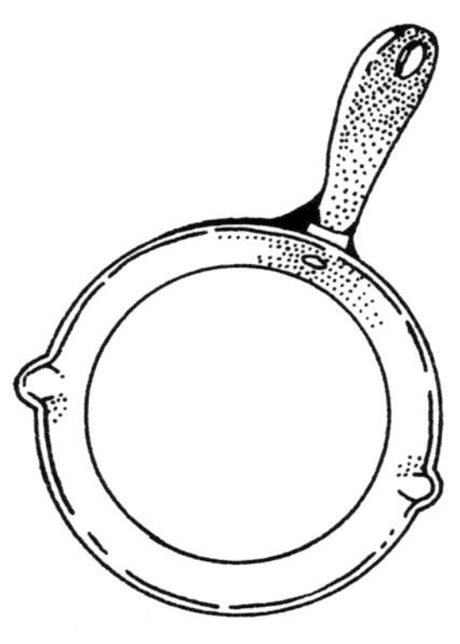

Potatoes	3 lbs (1.5 kg)
Lemon juice	1 Tbsp (15 mL)
Butter	3/4 cup (175 mL) melted
Onion	6 Tbsp (100 mL) grated
Salt	1 tsp (5 mL)
Pepper	1/2 tsp (2 mL)

1 Peel potatoes and cut into paper-thin slices. Drop into cold water with lemon juice to prevent discolouring.

2 Brush bottom and sides of a 9-inch by 3-inch (2-L) soufflé or casserole dish with butter. Drain potatoes and pat dry.

3 Place an overlapping layer of potatoes in bottom of dish. Brush with butter and sprinkle lightly with onion, salt and pepper. Repeat layers about three more times.

4 Pour remaining butter over the top and cover lightly with foil. Bake at 400°F (200°C) for 30 minutes. Remove from oven; cool and refrigerate.

Last minute preparation Bake, uncovered, for 30 minutes at 350°F (180°C), or until top is well browned. Unmold by inverting baking dish over warmed serving platter. Use a spatula to loosen the sides if necessary.

GREEN SALAD WITH GARLIC DRESSING

Egg white	1 small
Red wine vinegar	1/4 cup (50 mL)
Lemon juice	4 tsp (20 mL)
Salt	1 tsp (5 mL)
Pepper	1/4 tsp (1 mL)
Dry mustard	1/4 tsp (1 mL)
Olive oil	1 cup (250 mL)
Garlic	1 clove, minced
Salad greens — Boston, iceberg or leaf lettuce, endive, romaine, spinach	8 cups (2 L), assortment

1 Beat egg white until frothy. Add vinegar, lemon juice, salt, pepper, mustard, oil and garlic. Mix well, cover and refrigerate.

2 Wash salad greens and tear into bite-sized pieces. Wrap in paper towels and store in plastic bag in refrigerator.

Last minute preparation Toss salad greens in a bowl. Shake dressing well and add just enough to coat the greens.

CHERRIES JUBILEE

Pitted black cherries	2 14-oz (398-mL) cans
Sugar	1/2 cup (125 mL)
Kirsch or Cognac	1/2 cup (125 mL)
Cornstarch	2 Tbsp (25 mL)
Cognac or brandy	3/4 to 1 cup (175 to 250 mL)
French vanilla ice cream	2 quarts (2 L)

1 Drain cherries and reserve 1/2 cup (125 mL) of the juice.

2 Add sugar and Kirsch to drained cherries and store until serving time.

Last minute preparation Heat chafing dish. Drain cherries again and combine marinade with cornstarch. Put into warmed chafing dish and stir over medium-high heat until thickened, adding reserved cherry juice as needed. Add cherries and sprinkle with brandy. For a spectacular effect, turn lights down low and ignite brandy. Spoon the flaming mixture into the cherries until flames are extinguished. Serve over individual portions of vanilla ice cream.

TIME AND TEMPERATURE CHART

8:10	Broil	Crab and Bacon Rolls
8:15	350°F (180°C)	Veal Cordon Bleu Quiche Tarts
8:30	350°F (180°C)	Pommes Anna Ratatouille
8:50		Remove cover from Veal

German Menu

Hors d'oeuvres	Brandied Pâté
First Course	Hot Beer Soup
Main Course	Red Cabbage and Apple Salad
	Beef Rouladen
	Dilled Carrot Coins
	Onion-Potato Pancakes
Dessert	Black Forest Cake

Co-op Chart

Host/Hostess	Beef Rouladen
Couple A	Pâté, Onion-Potato Pancakes
Couple B	Dilled Carrot Coins, Black Forest Cake
Couple C	Hot Beer Soup, Red Cabbage Salad

BRANDIED PÂTÉ

Bacon	2 slices, chopped
Onion	1/2 small, chopped
Garlic	1 clove, minced
Chicken livers	1/2 lb (250 g)
Chicken stock	1 cup (250 mL)
Brandy	2 Tbsp (25 mL)
Ground allspice	pinch
Salt	1/4 tsp (1 mL)
Dried thyme	1/8 tsp (0.5 mL)
Pepper	1/8 tsp (0.5 mL)
Whipping cream	3 Tbsp (50 mL)
Crackers, Melba toast, pumpernickel bread	assortment

1 In a medium-sized skillet fry bacon, onion and garlic for 3 minutes.

2 Trim chicken livers and simmer in hot stock until cooked, 8 to 10 minutes. Drain.

3 Combine bacon, onion, garlic, livers, brandy, allspice, salt, thyme, pepper and cream in food processor or blender and purée until very smooth. Turn into a bowl, cover tightly and refrigerate for several hours.

Last minute preparation Serve at room temperature with Melba toast, crackers or pumpernickel bread.

HOT BEER SOUP

Fresh lemon	1
Beer	6 1/2 cups (1.625 L)
Whole cloves	4
Cinnamon stick	1 2-inch (5-cm) piece
Cornstarch	6 Tbsp (100 mL)
Eggs	4
Sugar	1/4 cup (50 mL)

1 Peel yellow rind from lemon in one or two large spirals.

2 In a large pot bring 6 cups (1.5 L) beer, lemon rind, cloves and cinnamon stick to a full boil. Cool and refrigerate.

3 Mix cornstarch with 1/2 cup (125 mL) beer and set aside.

Last minute preparation Bring soup to a full boil, add cornstarch mixture and return to the boil. In a large bowl, with an electric mixer beat eggs and sugar until frothy. Continue mixing with a whisk while slowly straining hot soup mixture into eggs. Serve hot.

RED CABBAGE AND APPLE SALAD

Red cabbage	1 medium
Cider vinegar	1/3 cup (75 mL)
Oil	1/4 cup (50 mL)
Sugar	2 Tbsp (25 mL)
Salt	1 tsp (5 mL)
Caraway seeds	1/2 tsp (2 mL)
Apple	1 medium

1 Remove tough outer leaves and shred cabbage as finely as possible until you have 6 cups (1.5 L).

2 In small saucepan combine vinegar, oil, sugar, salt and caraway seeds and stir over low heat until sugar dissolves. Pour over cabbage, toss thoroughly and marinate for an hour or more.

Last minute preparation Peel, core and grate apple. Add to cabbage and toss well.

BEEF ROULADEN

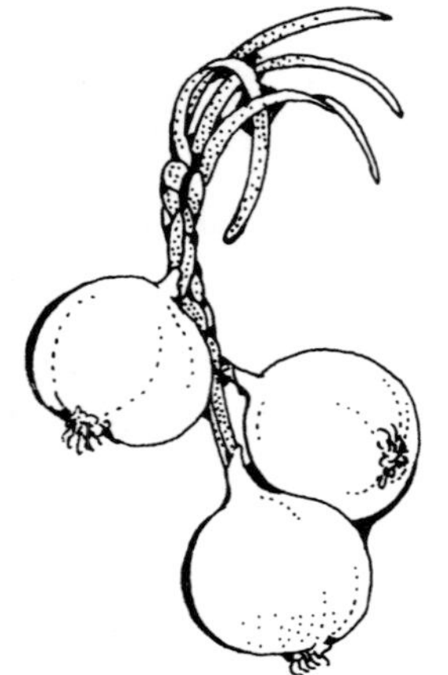

Onions	6
Oil	4 Tbsp (65 mL)
Garlic	3 cloves, minced
Fresh parsley	3 Tbsp (50 mL) chopped
Salt	1/8 tsp (0.5 mL)
Pepper	1/8 tsp (0.5 mL)
Ground thyme	1/8 tsp (0.5 mL)
Bread	3 slices
Beef stock	2 1/3 cups (575 mL)
Ground pork	1 1/2 lbs (750 g)
Eggs	2, lightly beaten
Beef rouladen (top or inside round steak)	10 slices, 4 inches x 6 inches (10 cm x 15 cm)
Prepared mustard	3 Tbsp (50 mL)
Bacon	10 slices
Large dill pickles	3, cut in quarters lengthwise
Tomato paste	2 Tbsp (25 mL)
Flour	4 Tbsp (65 mL)
Beer	2 bottles

1 Finely chop 2 onions and thinly slice remaining 4.

2 In a medium-sized frying pan heat 2 Tbsp (25 mL) oil and add chopped onions, garlic, parsley, salt, pepper and thyme. Fry until onion is transparent, then remove from heat.

3 Soak bread in 1/3 cup (75 mL) stock, then add to onion mixture with ground pork and eggs. Mix together well, then divide into 10 portions.

4 Lay beef slices on counter and top each with 1 tsp (5 mL) mustard, then one slice of bacon folded in a V shape, one portion of ground pork mixture spread along the centre and one dill pickle spear parallel to the pork mixture. Roll steak around filling and secure with a string to form rouladen.

5 Heat remaining oil in a frying pan and brown rouladens on all sides. Fit them snugly into a large ovenproof casserole.

6 To frying pan add sliced onions, tomato paste and flour and fry well while stirring.

7 Add beer and 2 cups (500 mL) stock and bring to a boil, stirring constantly. Pour over meat in casserole.

8 Bake, uncovered, at 350°F (180°C) for 30 minutes. If sauce does not cover rouladens, turn them once. Cool, cover and refrigerate.

9 When cold remove string.

Last minute preparation Reheat, uncovered, at 350°F (180°C) for 30 minutes. For this menu, because the oven will be full, reheat from 8:25 to 8:55 and store, covered, on warm stove top while potatoes are being cooked.

DILLED CARROT COINS

Carrots	2 lbs (1 kg)
Dried dill weed	2 tsp (10 mL)
Butter	1/3 cup (75 mL)

1 Peel carrots, slice diagonally and store in water.

Last minute preparation Steam or boil carrots in a small amount of water until just tender, approximately 10 minutes. Drain, leaving about 2 Tbsp (25 mL) water in the pot. Add dill weed and butter to carrots and shake to combine. Cover pot and place on warm stove top, not on an element, to keep warm until serving time. Pour into a serving dish and include the buttery sauce.

ONION-POTATO PANCAKES

Eggs	2
Flour	1/2 cup (125 mL)
Milk	1 cup (250 mL)
Salt	2 tsp (10 mL)
Pepper	1/2 tsp (2 mL)
Potatoes	4 large, peeled and cooked
Green onions	1/2 cup (125 mL) finely chopped
Butter	1/2 cup (125 mL) melted
Sour cream	1 1/2 cups (375 mL)

1 Combine eggs, flour, milk, salt and pepper. Finely grate cooked potatoes and combine with onions and egg mixture.

Last minute preparation Prepare eight 8-inch (20-cm) foil pie pans by putting 1 Tbsp (15 mL) melted butter in each. Stir potato mixture again and divide equally into pans. Bake at 400°F (200°C) for 15 minutes, shifting position of pans halfway through the cooking time. Remove from pans, fold in half and arrange on a platter. Serve with sour cream.

BLACK FOREST CAKE

Cake

Eggs	5
Sugar	2/3 cup (150 mL)
All-purpose flour	7/8 cup (225 mL) sifted
Cocoa	1/2 cup (125 mL)
Butter	3 Tbsp (50 mL) melted

Filling

Pitted black cherries	1 14-oz (398-mL) can
Cornstarch	1/4 cup (50 mL)
Sugar	1/3 cup (75 mL)
Kirsch liqueur	1/3 cup (75 mL)
Whipping cream	2 cups (500 mL)
Unsweetened chocolate	2 oz (60 g)
Glacé cherries	10

1 To make cake, combine eggs and sugar in a large mixing bowl. Beat at medium speed for about 5 minutes until they are tripled in volume, fluffy and light in colour.

2 Sift flour and cocoa together, then gently fold into eggs 1/3 at a time. Carefully add cooled melted butter.

3 Line three 8-inch (20-cm) pans with waxed paper. Grease and dust lightly with sifted cocoa. Divide batter equally into pans. Bake at 350°F (180°C) for 15 minutes, then remove and invert on cake racks. Remove waxed paper and cool.

4 For filling, drain cherry juice into saucepan. Combine cornstarch with 3 Tbsp (50 mL) water and add to juice. Cook over moderate heat until thickened. Cool, then add cherries.

5 Combine sugar with 1/3 cup (75 mL) water and boil for 5 minutes to make a syrup. Cool, then add Kirsch.

6 Whip the cream.

7 To assemble, put one cake layer on a serving plate and sprinkle with 1/3 of the Kirsch-flavoured syrup. Add a layer of whipped cream and half the cherries. Add the second cake layer, 1/3 of the syrup, whipped cream and remaining cherries. Top with last sponge layer and sprinkle with remaining syrup.

8 Frost top and sides with remaining cream and decorate with chocolate shavings made by running a vegetable peeler over chocolate at room temperature. Add glacé cherries on top. Refrigerate.

Last minute preparation Serve this masterpiece directly from the refrigerator.

TIME AND TEMPERATURE CHART

8:25	375°F (190°C)	Beef Rouladen
8:45	Stove top	Soup
8:50	Stove top	Dilled Carrot Coins
8:55	400°F (180°C)	Remove Rouladen from oven Potato Pancakes

Hawaiian Menu

Hors d'oeuvres	Teriyaki Banana Appetizers Fish and Fruit Kebobs
Main Course	Beef with Papaya Chicken with Ginger Green Beans Orientale Coconut Sweet Potatoes Curried Rice
Dessert	Coconut-Pineapple Ice Cream and Fresh Fruit

Co-op Chart

Host/Hostess	Beef with Papaya, Chicken with Ginger
Couple A	Teriyaki Banana Appetizers, Curried Rice
Couple B	Green Beans Orientale, Coconut-Pineapple Ice Cream and Fresh Fruit
Couple C	Fish and Fruit Kebobs, Coconut Sweet Potatoes

Note Because this menu includes two main dishes, the quantity of each dish has been reduced.

TERIYAKI BANANA APPETIZERS

Honey	1/3 cup (75 mL)
Soy sauce	1/2 cup (125 mL)
Dry sherry	3 Tbsp (50 mL)
Fresh ginger	1 piece, size of a quarter, finely minced
Garlic	1 small clove, finely minced
Bananas	4, firm
Cooked ham	8 thin slices

1. To make marinade, combine honey, soy sauce, sherry, ginger and garlic.
2. One or two hours before dinner, peel bananas and slice into 1-inch (2.5-cm) pieces. Marinate for one hour, turning or basting often.
3. Cut ham into strips 1-inch (2.5-cm) wide, wrap one piece around each banana slice and secure with a toothpick. Return to marinade, cover and refrigerate for 1/2 hour.

Last minute preparation Broil bananas, basting with marinade as needed, about 5 minutes. Serve hot.

FISH AND FRUIT KEBOBS

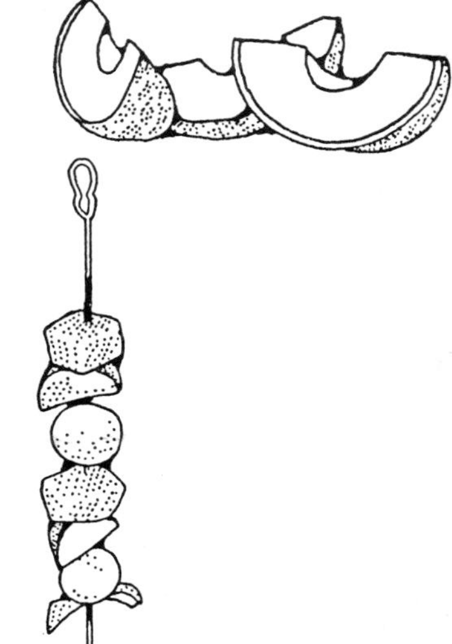

Green onion	1 Tbsp (15 mL) chopped
Lime juice	6 Tbsp (100 mL)
Honey	2 Tbsp (25 mL)
Salt	1/4 tsp (1 mL)
Swordfish or halibut steaks	1/2 lb (250 gl)
Cantaloupe melon	1 small
Kiwi fruit	4 to 5, peeled and quartered

1 In a medium-sized bowl combine green onions with lime juice, honey and salt.

2 Cut fish into 3/4-inch (2-cm) cubes and marinate in lime juice mixture. Cover and refrigerate at least 2 hours.

3 Peel melon, remove seeds and cut into 1-inch (2.5-cm) cubes or balls.

Last minute preparation Thread one piece each of melon, fish and kiwi on a wooden skewer. Broil, turning at least once, until the fish is cooked, about 4 to 5 minutes. Serve hot.

BEEF WITH PAPAYA

Green onions	6
Beef round steak	3 lbs (1.5 kg)
Fresh ginger	1/4 cup (50 mL) grated
Fresh papayas (or peaches)	3
Oil	1/4 cup (50 mL)
Soy sauce	1/4 cup (50 mL)
Oyster sauce	1/4 cup (50 mL)
Gin	1 Tbsp (15 mL)
Sugar	2 Tbsp (25 mL)
Water chestnuts	10, sliced
Cornstarch	2 Tbsp (25 mL)
Water	1/4 cup (50 mL)

1 Cut onions into 1-inch (2.5-cm) pieces. Slice beef into thin strips 2 inches (5 cm) long and mix with ginger.

2 Pare and seed papayas and cut into small chunks. Sprinkle with a little lemon juice and store in a tightly covered container.

Last minute preparation In large wok or skillet over high heat, heat oil and stir-fry onions for 5 minutes. Add meat and fry 3 more minutes. Reduce heat and stir in soy sauce, oyster sauce, gin, sugar and water chestnuts. Mix cornstarch and water together and add to beef. Cook, stirring constantly until sauce thickens. Gently stir in papayas and serve.

Clockwise: Duchess Potatoes (page 113); Spinach Crêpe Cups (page 111); Italian Asparagus (page 136); Duck Montmorency (page 112); Tomato and Cucumber Salad (page 114).

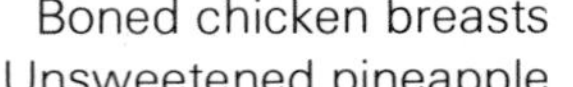

CHICKEN WITH GINGER

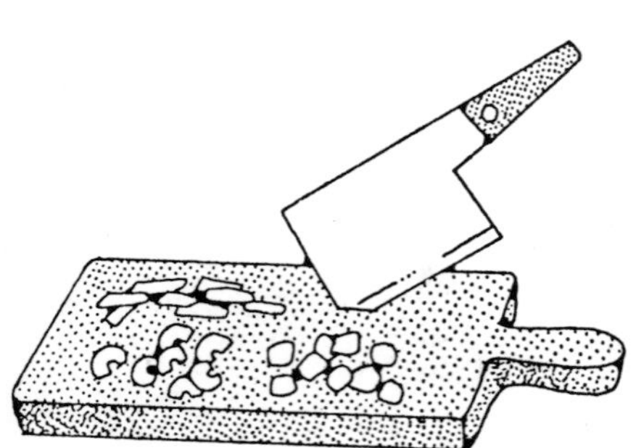

Boned chicken breasts	4 single
Unsweetened pineapple chunks	1 19-oz (540-mL) can
Salt	1 tsp (5 mL)
Pepper	1/4 tsp (1 mL)
Chicken stock	1 1/2 cups (375 mL)
Honey	1/3 cup (75 mL)
Soy sauce	1/3 cup (75 mL)
Oil	3 Tbsp (50 mL)
Fresh ginger	1/4 cup (50 mL) grated
Celery	3 ribs, sliced diagonally
Chili pepper flakes	1/4 tsp (1 mL)
Cornstarch	3 Tbsp (50 mL)
Macadamia or Brazil nuts	1/2 cup (125 mL) coarsely chopped

1 Discard skin from chicken and cut meat into 2-inch (5-cm) cubes.

2 Drain pineapple and combine juice with salt, pepper, stock, honey and soy sauce.

3 In frying pan heat oil and cook chicken until opaque, then remove from pan. Add ginger, celery and chili flakes and sauté for 3 minutes, then add juice mixture. Combine cornstarch with 3 Tbsp (50 mL) water and add to sauce, stirring until sauce thickens. Mix in chicken and pineapple chunks. Transfer to a covered 2-quart (2-L) casserole. Cool and refrigerate.

Last minute preparation Bake, covered, at 350°F (180°C) for 40 minutes. Sprinkle with nuts at serving time.

GREEN BEANS ORIENTALE

Green beans	2 lbs (1 kg)
Salt	1 Tbsp (15 mL)
Soy sauce	1/3 cup (75 mL)
Sugar	2 tsp (10 mL)
Pepper	1/2 tsp (2 mL)

1 Wash beans and slice into 2-inch (5-cm) pieces. Bring 2 quarts (2 L) water to a boil. Add salt and green beans. Return to a boil and cook, uncovered, for 10 minutes.

2 Drain and immediately immerse in cold water to stop cooking process. Drain, cover and refrigerate.

Last minute preparation In a medium-sized pot heat beans, soy sauce, sugar and pepper over medium heat until piping hot, about 8 minutes.

COCONUT SWEET POTATOES

Sweet potatoes	6 large
Butter	1/3 cup (75 mL) melted
Flaked unsweetened coconut	1 cup (250 mL)

1 Cook potatoes in large pot of boiling salted water until tender, about 40 minutes. Drain, cool and peel.

2 Cut each potato in half and arrange in an ovenproof casserole. Brush with melted butter and sprinkle with coconut. Cover and refrigerate.

Last minute preparation Bake, uncovered, at 350°F (180°C) until browned, about 15 minutes.

CURRIED RICE

Long grain rice	2 cups (500 mL)
Oil	1/3 cup (75 mL)
Onion	1 large, chopped
Curry powder	4 tsp (20 mL)
Bay leaf	1
Whole cloves	2
Salt	1 1/2 tsp (7 mL)
Raisins	2/3 cup (150 mL)
Slivered almonds	1/4 cup (50 mL)
Chicken stock	4 cups (1 L)

1 Rinse rice under running cold water until the water runs clear.

2 In a medium-sized saucepan heat oil and sauté onion, curry powder, bay leaf and cloves until onion is transparent. Add rice and continue cooking for 4 more minutes. Add salt, raisins and almonds, then remove from heat and cool.

Last minute preparation Reheat rice, add stock and bring to a boil. Cover, reduce heat to a low simmer and cook for 15 minutes. Turn off heat and let sit for 10 minutes. Remove bay leaf and cloves and fluff with a fork.

COCONUT-PINEAPPLE ICE CREAM AND FRESH FRUIT

Crushed pineapple	1 cup (250 mL) drained
Whipping cream	1 1/4 cups (300 mL), chilled
Vanilla extract	1/2 tsp (2 mL)
Almond extract	1/4 tsp (1 mL)
Sugar	2/3 cup (175 mL)
Egg whites	3
Shredded coconut	3 Tbsp (50 mL)
Fresh fruit — pineapple, orange, papaya, kiwi, mango, banana, watermelon, coconut	assortment

1 Purée pineapple in blender or food processor and drain well.

2 Whip cream and vanilla and almond extract until firm. Boil sugar and 2/3 cup (175 mL) water for five minutes. Whip egg whites until stiff and gradually add hot sugar syrup, beating until meringue is thick and cool. Fold in the cream and pour into refrigerator trays. Freeze until firm around the edges.

3 Toast coconut very carefully under broiler, until golden.

4 Remove ice cream from freezer and fold in pineapple purée and coconut. Return ice cream to the trays and freeze until firm.

5 Slice fresh pineapple and remove peel and centre core. Break coconut into pieces with a hammer. Store in separate covered containers.

Last minute preparation Close to dinner time, peel and slice remaining fruit except for the banana and arrange on a tray with the pineapple and coconut. Spoon ice cream into serving dishes and store in freezer. Add sliced banana to tray of fruit just before serving.

TIME AND TEMPERATURE CHART

8:00	Broil	Teriyaki Banana Appetizers
8:10	Broil	Fish and Fruit Kebobs
8:20	350°F (180°C)	Chicken with Ginger
8:40	350°F (180°C)	Curried Rice
8:45	350°F (180°C)	Coconut Sweet Potatoes
8:45	Stove top	Beef with Papaya
8:50	Stove top	Green Beans

Italian Menu #1

First Course	Minestrone Soup
Second Course	Fettuccine with Spinach and Cheese
Main Course	Chicken Cacciatore
	Stuffed Eggplant
	Italian Asparagus
	Romaine Salad
Dessert	Spumone

Co-op Chart

Host/Hostess	Chicken Cacciatore
Couple A	Minestrone Soup, Stuffed Eggplant
Couple B	Fettuccine with Spinach and Cheese, Italian Asparagus
Couple C	Romaine Salad, Spumone

MINESTRONE SOUP

Oil	3 Tbsp (50 mL)
Garlic	1 large clove, minced
Carrots	3, chopped
Onion	1 large, chopped
Turnip (rutabaga)	1 very small, finely chopped
Potato	1 large, finely chopped
Celery	3 ribs, finely chopped
Beef stock	6 cups (1.5 L)
Leek	1 medium
Cabbage	1 1/2 cups (375 mL) shredded
Plum tomatoes	1 14-oz (398-mL) can, drained
Macaroni	1 cup (250 mL)
Salt	1 to 2 tsp (5 to 10 mL)
Pepper	1 tsp (5 mL)
Parmesan cheese	3/4 cup (175 mL) grated

1 In a heavy saucepan heat oil and garlic and add carrots, onion, turnip, potatoes and celery. Sauté over moderate heat until vegetables begin to soften, about 10 minutes. Add hot stock, cover pan and simmer over low heat until vegetables are tender, about 20 minutes.

2 Clean leek and slice only white part. Add leek, cabbage and tomatoes to soup and return to a boil. Add macaroni and simmer for 20 minutes. Cool and refrigerate.

Last minute preparation Simmer soup, uncovered, over low heat for 10 to 15 minutes. Season with salt and pepper to taste. Serve grated Parmesan cheese separately.

FETTUCCINE WITH SPINACH AND CHEESE

Fresh spinach	10 oz (280 g)
Butter	6 Tbsp (100 mL)
Garlic	1 clove, minced
Onion	1 small, chopped
Flour	3 Tbsp (50 mL)
Milk	1 1/2 cups (375 mL)
Cayenne pepper	pinch
Ground nutmeg	pinch
Pepper	1/2 tsp (2 mL)
Salt	1 Tbsp (15 mL)
Oil	2 tsp (10 mL)
Fettuccine noodles	12 oz (375 g)
Parmesan cheese	3/4 cup (175 mL) grated
Mozzarella cheese	3/4 cup (175 mL) grated

1 Wash spinach well, shake to discard water and cook in 1 Tbsp (15 mL) water until wilted. Drain well and squeeze to extract all moisture, then chop finely. Cover and refrigerate.

2 In a medium-sized saucepan melt 4 Tbsp (75 mL) butter and sauté garlic and onion until onion is transparent. Add flour, stirring well until mixture bubbles. Gradually add milk, stirring until thick. Add cayenne, nutmeg and pepper, then remove from heat. Cover and refrigerate.

Last minute preparation In a large pot boil 4 quarts (4 L) water. Add 1 Tbsp (15 mL) salt and 2 tsp (10 mL) oil. Add fettuccine and cook at full boil for 7 to 9 minutes. Meanwhile heat white sauce and stir in the cheese until almost melted. Add chopped spinach and heat thoroughly, but do not boil.

When fettuccine is cooked *al dente*, drain and rinse quickly with cold water, then with warm water to reheat noodles. Drain thoroughly and toss with 2 Tbsp (25 mL) butter. Serve on individual plates topped with spinach and cheese sauce.

CHICKEN CACCIATORE

Chicken breasts and/or legs	12
Flour	1/2 cup (125 mL)
Butter	4 Tbsp (65 mL)
Oil	6 Tbsp (100 mL)
Onions	2 medium, chopped
Garlic	2 cloves, minced
Fresh mushrooms	1/2 lb (250 g), sliced
Green peppers	2 large, seeded and diced
Dried oregano	2 tsp (10 mL)
Fresh parsley	2 tsp (10 mL)
Salt	1 1/2 tsp (7 mL)
Pepper	1/2 tsp (2 mL)
Plum tomatoes	1 19-oz (540-mL) can
Dry sherry	1 1/2 cups (375 mL)

1 Wash chicken pieces, pat dry and coat with flour.

2 In a large heavy skillet heat butter and oil over medium heat and brown chicken pieces, 15 minutes for white meat and 25 minutes for dark meat. Transfer to an ovenproof casserole.

3 Add onions, garlic, mushrooms, green peppers, oregano and parsley to skillet and sauté until tender.

4 Add salt, pepper, tomatoes and sherry to skillet and stir well. Pour sauce over chicken pieces in casserole. Cool, cover tightly, and refrigerate.

Last minute preparation Bake, covered, at 350°F (180°C) for one hour, basting occasionally.

STUFFED EGGPLANT

Eggplants	4 medium
Oil	2 Tbsp (25 mL)
Ricotta cheese	1/2 cup (125 mL)
Parmesan cheese	6 Tbsp (100 mL) grated
Fresh parsley	2 Tbsp (25 mL) chopped
Garlic	1 clove, minced
Egg	1
Soft bread crumbs	2/3 cup (150 mL)
Dry bread crumbs	1/3 cup (75 mL)
Butter	2 Tbsp (25 mL) melted

1 Cut eggplants in half lengthwise, sprinkle with 2 tsp (10 mL) salt and drain in a colander for 30 minutes. Rinse with cold water and pat dry. Scoop out the centre seeded portion and finely chop removed pulp.

2 Brush top of eggplants with a generous amount of oil and bake at 350°F (180°C) for about 15 to 20 minutes until pulp is softened.

3 Remove from oven and scoop out pulp, leaving a thin shell.

4 To make stuffing, mix softened pulp with chopped unbaked pulp, Ricotta cheese, 4 Tbsp (75 mL) Parmesan cheese, 1 Tbsp (15 mL) parsley, garlic, egg and soft bread crumbs. Mix well and stuff into eggplant shells.

5 Combine dry bread crumbs, 2 Tbsp (25 mL) Parmesan cheese, remaining parsley, and butter and sprinkle top of stuffed eggplant. Place in a buttered baking dish, cover and refrigerate.

Last minute preparation Bake, uncovered, at 350°F (180°C) for 30 minutes.

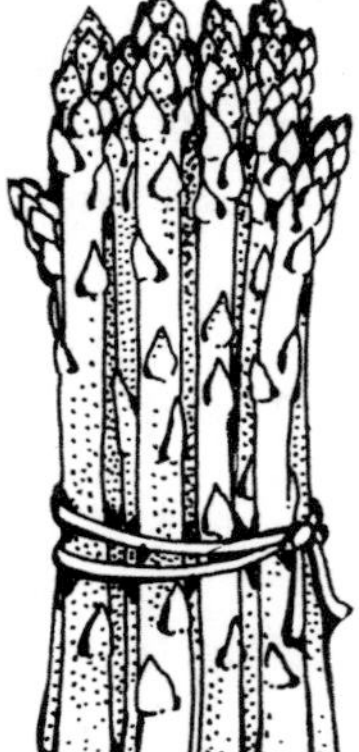

ITALIAN ASPARAGUS

Fresh asparagus	36 stalks
Prosciutto (Italian ham)	12 thin slices
Parmesan cheese	1/3 cup (75 mL) grated

1 Wash asparagus well. Snap off tough ends by bending the stalks. Cook in boiling salted water until just barely tender, then drain.

2 Wrap 1 piece of prosciutto around three stalks of asparagus and fasten with a toothpick.

3 Butter the bottom of a baking dish and lay bundles of asparagus in a single layer. Sprinkle with cheese. Cover and refrigerate.

Last minute preparation Bake, covered, at 350°F (180°C) for 15 minutes.

ROMAINE SALAD

Romaine lettuce	2 medium heads
Leaf lettuce	2 heads
Bermuda onion	1, thinly sliced
Olive oil	3/4 cup (175 mL)
Wine vinegar	3 Tbsp (50 mL)
Salt	1 tsp (5 mL)
Pepper	1/2 tsp (2 mL)
Dried basil	1/2 tsp (2 mL)
Canned artichoke hearts	3, coarsley chopped

1 Discard outside leaves from romaine and leaf lettuce and wash thoroughly. Tear into bite-sized pieces, wrap in paper towels and store in plastic bag in refrigerator.

2 Mix oil, vinegar, salt, pepper and basil and taste to correct seasoning. Store in a jar.

Last minute preparation Toss lettuce, onion, and artichoke with dressing and mix well.

SPUMONE

Sugar	1 cup (250 mL)
Water	1 cup (250 mL)
Egg yolks	9, at room temperature
Semi-sweet chocolate	2 oz (50 g), melted over hot water
Rum	1 tsp (5 mL)
Orange liqueur	1 tsp (5 mL)
Orange rind	1 tsp (5 mL) grated
Shelled pistachios	4 Tbsp (75 mL) chopped
Almond extract	1/2 tsp (2 mL)
Whipping cream	2 cups (500 mL)

Note Start this recipe one day in advance.

1 Combine 1 cup (250 mL) sugar and water in a medium-sized pot and stir over high heat until sugar dissolves. Boil, without stirring, until syrup registers 220°F (115°C) on a thermometer., in about 20 minutes.

2 In the interim, beat egg yolks at high speed until fluffy and very light, about 10 minutes. When syrup has reached correct temperature, add it to egg yolks in a fine stream while beating continuously. Keep beating until mixture forms peaks that are firm and has cooled to room temperature, about 10 minutes.

3 Divide into 3 bowls. Into the first, fold in cooled chocolate and rum, the refrigerate.

4 To the second, add liqueur and grated orange rind, then refrigerate.

5 To the last, add pistachios and almond extract and refrigerate.

6 With chilled beaters beat cream until stiff and fold an equal amount into each bowl. Put bowls into freezer.

7 Lightly oil a large mold. When the creams are almost frozen, remove from freezer and spoon mixtures into the mold in a random fashion. Swirl quickly with a knife, cutting down through the centre. Return to the freezer.

Last minute preparation Remove spumone from mold, arrange on a serving plate and return to freezer. Serve by slicing into wedges.

TIME AND TEMPERATURE CHART

8:20	350°F (180°C)	Chicken Cacciatore
8:45	Stove top	Soup
8:50	350°F (180°C)	Stuffed Eggplant
8:55	Stove top	Spinach Sauce
		Fettucine
9:10	350°F (180°C)	Italian Asparagus

Italian Menu #2

Hors d'oeuvres	Prosciutto Sandwiches
First Course	Tonnato
Main Course	Veal Scallopine al Marsala
	Manicotti Florentine
	Mixed Vegetables
Salad Course	Caesar Salad
Dessert	Chilled Zabaglione Cream

Co-op Chart

Host/Hostess	Veal Scallopine
Couple A	Tonnato, Mixed Vegetables
Couple B	Prosciutto Sandwiches, Chilled Zabaglione Cream
Couple C	Manicotti Florentine, Caesar Salad

PROSCIUTTO SANDWICHES

Prosciutto (Italian ham)	8 slices, very thin
Gorgonzola or blue cheese	1/3 lb (175 g), at room temperature
Sandwich bread	16 thin slices
Butter	1/2 cup (125 mL), approximately

1 Chop prosciutto and combine with cheese. Spread over 8 slices of bread and top with remaining bread. Trim off crusts.

2 Butter outside of sandwiches and stack between layers of foil or plastic wrap. Wrap and refrigerate or freeze.

Last minute preparation Grill sandwiches over low heat or carefully broil in oven until both sides are crisp and brown. The cheese should be melted. Cut each sandwich into quarters and serve hot.

TONNATO

Tuna	1 7-oz (184-g) can, drained
Onion	1 tsp (5 mL) grated
Lemon juice	1 Tbsp (15 mL)
Anchovy fillets	1 2-oz (50-g) can
Capers	2 tsp (10 mL) drained
Mayonnaise	1 cup (250 mL)
Pepper	1/4 tsp (1 mL)
Hard-boiled eggs	8
Lettuce leaves	8
Fresh parsley	8 sprigs
Tomatoes	2, cut in wedges

1 Combine tuna, onion, lemon juice, 4 anchovy fillets and capers. Process in blender or food processor until smooth. Add mayonnaise and pepper.

2 Cut eggs in half lengthwise and place, cut side down, on a large platter. Coat each egg with tuna mixture and decorate with remaining anchovy fillets. Cover well and refrigerate.

Last minute preparation On individual plates arrange eggs on lettuce leaves and garnish with parsley and tomato wedges.

VEAL SCALLOPINE AL MARSALA

Veal scallops	10 4-oz (125-g) slices, 1/2 inch (1 cm) thick
Flour	1/4 cup (50 mL)
Ground nutmeg	1/8 tsp (0.5 mL)
Paprika	1/8 tsp (0.5 mL)
Pepper	1/8 tsp (0.5 mL)
Oil	1/4 cup (50 mL)
Butter	2 Tbsp (25 mL)
Fresh mushrooms	1/2 lb (250 g), sliced
Lemon juice	1 Tbsp (15 mL)
Chicken stock	1/2 cup (125 mL)
Light cream	1 cup (250 mL)
Marsala wine or sherry	1/2 cup (125 mL)
Fresh parsley	2 Tbsp (25 mL) chopped

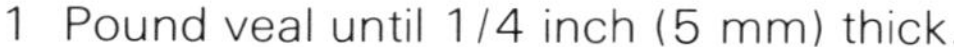

1 Pound veal until 1/4 inch (5 mm) thick.

2 Combine flour, nutmeg, paprika and pepper.

3 In a large heavy frying pan heat oil and butter over medium-high heat. Dredge veal in seasoned flour to coat evenly and sauté approximately one minute on each side. Remove to large oven-proof baking dish. Reserve seasoned flour.

4 When all the veal has been cooked and transferred, add mushrooms and lemon juice to frying pan and sauté briefly. Distribute over veal in baking dish.

5 Sprinkle reserved seasoned flour into frying pan and stir quickly. Add chicken stock, cream and wine, continuing to stir and cook.

6 When sauce is smooth and slightly thickened, pour over veal and mushrooms. Cool, cover and refrigerate.

Last minute preparation Bake, covered, at 300°F (150°C) for 30 minutes. If sauce is too thick, add a little wine. Sprinkle top with chopped parsley.

MANICOTTI FLORENTINE

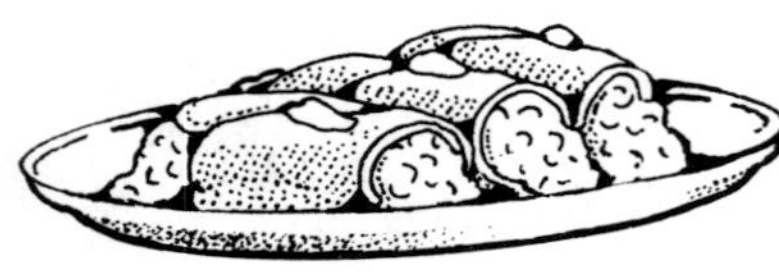

Fresh spinach	10 oz (280 g)
Ricotta or small curd cottage cheese	1 1/2 lbs (750 g)
Mozzarella cheese	8 oz (250 g), grated
Parmesan cheese	1/2 cup (125 mL) grated
Eggs	2
Ground nutmeg	pinch
Salt	3 1/2 tsp (17 mL)
Pepper	1/8 tsp (0.5 mL)
Thick spaghetti sauce	1 28-oz (796-mL) can
Dried basil	1/2 tsp (2 mL)
Tomato juice	1/2 cup (125 mL)
Oil	1 Tbsp (15 mL)
Manicotti pasta	9 oz (250 g)

1 Wash spinach well and cook in 1 Tbsp (15 mL) water. Drain well and chop.

2 To spinach add Ricotta, Mozzarella and Parmesan cheese, eggs, nutmeg, 1/2 tsp (2 mL) salt and pepper and mix well. Set aside.

3 Combine spaghetti sauce, basil and tomato juice and spread 1 1/2 cups (375 mL) in 9-inch by 13-inch (3.5-L) pan.

4 To 6 quarts (6 L) boiling water add 3 tsp (15 mL) salt and 1 Tbsp (15 mL) oil. Cook 8 manicotti at a time, being careful not to overcook. Remove from water, rinse in cool water and drain.

5 Stuff each manicotti with spinach mixture and arrange in single layer in prepared pan. Cover with the remaining spaghetti sauce and sprinkle with 2 Tbsp (25 mL) Parmesan cheese. Cover with foil and refrigerate.

Last minute preparation Bake, covered, at 300°F (150°C) for 45 minutes. Remove from oven and let stand 10 minutes before serving.

MIXED VEGETABLES

Broccoli	2 bunches
Carrots	8 small
Leeks	4
Fresh mushrooms	1/2 lb (250 g)
Oil	3 Tbsp (50 mL)
Garlic	1 clove, minced
Fresh parsley	2 Tbsp (25 mL) chopped
Salt	1 tsp (5 mL)
Pepper	1/4 tsp (1 mL)
Dried savory	1 1/2 tsp (7 mL)
Lemon juice	2 Tbsp (25 mL)

1 Wash broccoli and cut florets and stems into bite-sized pieces. Cut carrots into long slivers and store together with broccoli.

2 Wash leeks well and slice white part only. Wash mushrooms and cut in half, if large. Store leeks and mushrooms together.

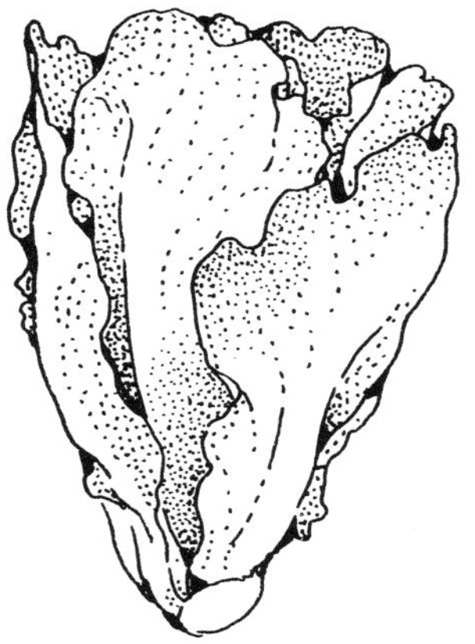

Last minute preparation Steam carrots and broccoli together until just cooked, about 8 minutes. Meanwhile heat oil in large frying pan and sauté leeks, mushrooms and garlic for 2 minutes. Add drained broccoli and carrots, parsley, salt, pepper, savory and lemon juice. Cook and stir until hot and well combined.

CAESAR SALAD

Garlic	2 large cloves
Salt	1/8 tsp (0.5 mL)
Pepper	1/8 tsp (0.5 mL)
Egg yolk	1
Anchovy paste	1/2 tsp (2 mL)
Lemon juice	4 tsp (20 mL)
Dry mustard	1/8 tsp (0.5 mL)
Prepared mustard	1/4 tsp (1 mL)
Tabasco sauce	3 drops
Worcestershire sauce	1/2 tsp (2 mL)
Wine vinegar	1/4 tsp (1 mL)
Olive oil	3 Tbsp (50 mL)
Romaine lettuce	2 large heads
Bacon	4 slices
Parmesan cheese	2 Tbsp (25 mL) grated
Croutons	3/4 cup (175 mL), or to taste

1 To make dressing, mash garlic with salt and pepper. Add egg yolk and cream well. Combine anchovy paste and lemon juice and add to egg yolk mixture. Add mustards, Tabasco, Worcestershire sauce, vinegar and oil and combine well. Cover and set aside.

2 Wash romaine lettuce and tear into bite-sized pieces. Wrap in paper towels, put in plastic bag and refrigerate.

3 Cook bacon until crisp, then crumble and set aside.

Last minute preparation Put romaine lettuce in a salad bowl and toss with just enough dressing to moisten. Add Parmesan, bacon and croutons, tossing after each addition.

CHILLED ZABAGLIONE CREAM

Sugar	1/2 cup (125 mL)
Unflavoured gelatin	1 envelope
Marsala wine or dry sherry	2/3 cup (150 mL)
Eggs	4, separated
Lemon rind	1/2 tsp (2 mL) finely grated
Vanilla extract	1 tsp (5 mL)
Whipping cream	1 1/3 cups (325 mL)
Semi-sweet chocolate	1 oz (30 g)

1 In top of double boiler, mix 4 Tbsp (75 mL) sugar and gelatin. Stir in Marsala or sherry.

2 With electric mixer beat egg yolks until light and lemon coloured and stir into gelatin mixture. Cook over hot water, stirring constantly, until thickened. Remove from heat and add lemon rind and vanilla. Cool.

3 Whip cream until stiff and fold into egg yolk mixture.

4 Beat egg whites until stiff, adding remaining 3 Tbsp (50 mL) sugar, 1 Tbsp (15 mL) at a time.

5 Fold egg whites gently into the gelatin and spoon into parfait or dessert dishes. Chill at least 1 hour.

6 Garnish with chocolate curls made by running a knife or vegetable peeler over a piece of chocolate at room temperature.

Last minute preparations This variation on a traditional dessert is a refreshing finale to this Italian night. Serve well chilled.

TIME AND TEMPERATURE CHART

8:10	Broil	Prosciutto Sandwiches
8:15	300°F (150°C)	Manicotti Florentine
8:40	300°F (150°C)	Veal Scallopine
8:50	Stove top	Mixed Vegetables
9:00		Remove Manicotti Florentine

Mexican Menu

Hors d'oeuvres	Sangria and/or Margarita Cocktails
	Salsa Cruda and Tortilla Chips
Main Course	Tacos with Sour Cream
	Spanish Rice
	Chicken Mole
	Corn with Cream
	Green Peas Mexican Style
Dessert	Almendrado

Co-op Chart

Host/Hostess	Tacos with Sour Cream, Chicken Mole
Couple A	Sangria/Margarita, Corn with Cream
Couple B	Salsa Cruda, Green Peas
Couple C	Spanish Rice, Almendrado

Note Because this menu includes two main course dishes, the quantity for each dish has been reduced.

SANGRIA

Lemon	1, thinly sliced
Orange	1, thinly sliced
Ripe peaches	2, pitted and cubed
Sugar	1/2 cup (125 mL), approximately
Dry red wine	2 26-oz (750-mL) bottles
Brandy	1/4 cup (50 mL)
Club soda	1 26-oz (750-mL) bottle

1 Combine lemon, orange and peaches with half of the sugar and place in a large pitcher. Add wine and mix well. Chill.

This was originally a Spanish drink, but it is so popular in Mexico that they have adopted it as their own.

Last minute preparation Add brandy and taste. Add more sugar, if desired, and mix well. Add club soda and plenty of ice and serve in a punch bowl.

MARGARITA COCKTAIL

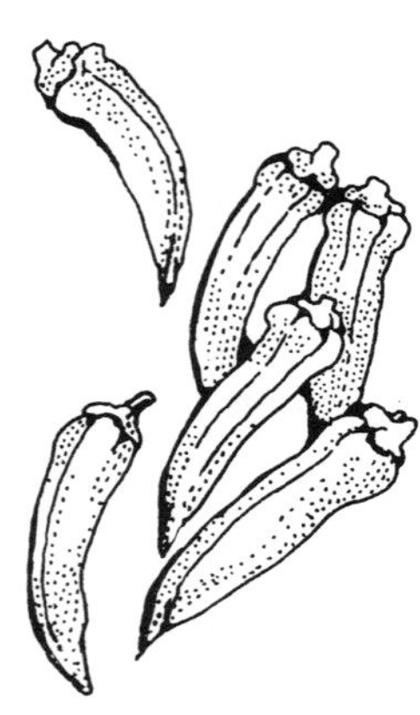

Lemon	1
Salt	1/2 cup (125 mL), approximately
White tequila	1 to 1 1/2 oz (30 to 40 mL)
Cointreau or Triple Sec liqueur	1/2 oz (15 mL)
Fresh lemon or lime juice	1 oz (30 mL)

Last minute preparation Rub the rim of a chilled glass with a piece of lemon, then turn in a dish of loose salt to encrust the rim. Combine Tequila, Cointreau and lemon juice with crushed ice in a cocktail shaker. Shake until frothy and strain into prepared glass. Serve immediately. These directions are for one drink and can be increased according to demand.

SALSA CRUDA WITH TORTILLA CHIPS

Fresh or canned mild green chilies	4
Tomatoes	3 large, peeled and finely chopped
Green onions	3 small, chopped
Vinegar	4 tsp (20 mL)
Garlic	2 cloves, minced
Salt	1/2 tsp (2 mL)
Pepper	1/4 tsp (1 mL)
Frozen tortillas	1 package (substitute snack tortilla chips if necessary)

Note Prepare the salsa cruda one day in advance to allow flavours to blend.

1 Wearing rubber gloves, seed and finely chop chilies.

2 Combine chilies, tomatoes, onions, vinegar, garlic, salt and pepper. Cover and refrigerate for 24 hours.

3 Frozen tortillas can be bought in specialty shops, or ask a local Mexican restaurant for the source of their supply. Thaw as many as needed and keep the rest frozen.

4 To make tortilla chips, cut a thawed tortilla into quarters. Close to serving time, heat oil to 425°F (220°C) and deep fry 6 to 8 wedges at a time. They are finished when no more moisture escapes from them and they are a light golden brown, about 1 1/2 minutes. Drain on paper towels and sprinkle with salt. Packaged snack tortilla chips can be substituted.

Last minute preparation Serve chilled salsa cruda with tortilla chips.

TACOS WITH SOUR CREAM

Onion	1/2 cup (125 mL) chopped
Garlic	1 large clove, minced
Oil	2 Tbsp (25 mL)
Chili powder	4 Tbsp (65 mL)
Dried oregano	1/2 tsp (2 mL)
Salt	1 tsp (5 mL)
Tomatoes	2, chopped
Stock or water	1/2 cup (125 mL)
Mild green chilies	4
Mild Cheddar cheese	1 lb (500 g)
Frozen or canned tortillas	12
Cooking oil	2 cups (500 mL)
Sour cream	2 1/2 cups (625 mL)

1 Sauté onion and garlic in oil until soft, then add chili powder, oregano, salt, tomatoes and stock. Simmer for 10 minutes. Cool and set aside.

2 Wearing rubber gloves, seed and finely chop chilies and add to chili sauce.

3 Cut cheese into 12 fingers.

4 Close to dinner time dip a tortilla into hot oil for about 30 seconds, then drain on paper towelling. Place one finger of cheese and 2 Tbsp (25 mL) chili sauce along the centre and roll up. Place seam-side down in a baking dish.

5 Prepare remaining tortillas, working quickly. Cover pan and set aside until baking time.

Last minute preparation Pour sour cream over tacos and bake, uncovered, at 350°F (180°C) for 30 minutes.

SPANISH RICE

Long grain rice	2 cups (500 mL)
Oil	2 Tbsp (25 mL)
Onion	1, chopped
Garlic	2 cloves, minced
Tomato sauce	1 1/2 cups (375 mL)
Salt	1 tsp (5 mL)
Chicken stock	3 cups (750 mL)

1 Rinse rice under cold running water until water runs clear. Drain well.

2 In a medium-sized saucepan heat oil and sauté onion and garlic until soft but not brown. Add rice and stir and cook for 3 minutes. Put into a covered ovenproof casserole.

Last minute preparation To the rice in casserole, stir in tomato sauce, salt and boiling stock. Cover and cook at 350°F (180°C) for approximately 40 minutes. This can also be cooked on the stove top, over low heat, for 25 to 30 minutes.

CHICKEN MOLE

Oil	4 Tbsp (75 mL)
Chicken breasts and/or legs	10 small
Onion	1, chopped
Garlic	1 large clove, minced
Green pepper	3/4 cup (175 mL) chopped
Canned tomatoes	2 cups (500 mL) drained
Chili powder	2 Tbsp (25 mL)
Chicken stock	2 1/2 cups (625 mL)
Ground allspice	1/2 tsp (2 mL)
Ground cinnamon	1/4 tsp (1 mL)
Salt	1/2 tsp (2 mL)
Pepper	1/4 tsp (1 mL)
Orange rind	1 Tbsp (15 mL)
Unsweetened chocolate	2 oz (60 g)

1 In a heavy saucepan heat the oil and brown the chicken, 15 minutes for white meat and 25 minutes for dark meat. Transfer to ovenproof casserole as pieces are cooked. Cover and refrigerate.

2 Sauté onion and garlic for 5 minutes, then add green pepper, tomatoes and chili powder and cook, stirring, for 5 minutes.

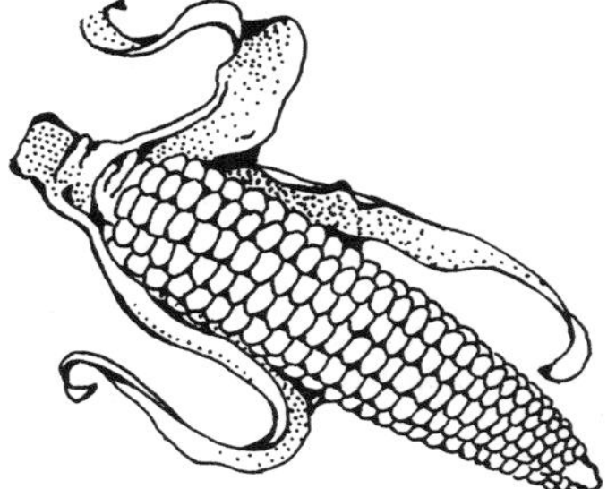

3 Add stock, allspice, cinnamon, salt, pepper and orange rind. Lower heat and simmer gently for 10 minutes.

4 Break up chocolate and add to sauce, stirring until melted.

5 Cool sauce and pour over chicken. Cover and refrigerate.

Last minute preparation Bake, covered, at 350°F (180°C) for 1 hour, basting if necessary.

CORN WITH CREAM

Mild green chilies	3
Butter	6 Tbsp (100 mL)
Onion	1 small, chopped
Frozen corn kernels	4 cups (1 L)
Salt	1 tsp (5 mL)
Pepper	1/2 tsp (2 mL)
Cream cheese	4 oz (125 g)
Muenster cheese	1/2 cup (125 mL) grated
Light cream	3/4 cup (175 mL)

1 Wearing rubber gloves, seed and finely chop chilies.

2 In a skillet melt butter and sauté onion until soft. Add chilies, corn, salt and pepper and sauté briefly. Pour into an ovenproof serving dish.

Last minute preparation Cut cream cheese into small pieces and combine with Muenster cheese and cream. Stir into corn, cover and bake at 350°F (180°C) for 15 minutes. Stir occasionally to melt cheese. Serve hot.

GREEN PEAS MEXICAN STYLE

Butter	2 Tbsp (25 mL)
Garlic	2 cloves, whole
Onion	1 small, chopped
Tomatoes	2 medium, peeled and chopped
Frozen green peas	1 1/2 lbs (750 g)
Dried basil	1/2 tsp (2 mL)
Salt	1/2 tsp (2 mL)
Lettuce leaves	6
Water	1/3 cup (75 mL)

1 Melt butter and sauté garlic cloves until golden, then discard garlic.

2 Add onion and tomatoes and sauté over high heat until soft.

3 Add frozen peas, basil, salt, lettuce leaves and water and cook just until peas are thawed. Put in ovenproof serving dish.

Last minute preparation Bake, covered, at 350°F (180°C) for 20 minutes, or until heated through.

ALMENDRADO

Sugar	1 cup (250 mL)
Unflavoured gelatin	1 envelope
Water	1 1/4 cups (300 mL)
Egg whites	5
Almond extract	1/4 tsp (1 mL)
Lemon peel	1/4 tsp (1 mL) grated
Almonds	1/2 cup (125 mL) finely chopped
Red food colouring	2 drops
Green food colouring	2 drops
Custard	
Egg yolks	3
Sugar	2 Tbsp (25 mL)
Salt	pinch
Lemon peel	1/4 tsp (1 mL) grated
Milk	1 cup (250 mL)
Whipping cream	1/2 cup (125 mL)
Vanilla extract	1/2 tsp (2 mL)

1 In a small saucepan combine sugar, gelatin and water. Stir over low heat until gelatin and sugar have dissolved.

2 Beat egg whites and almond extract with electric mixer until soft peaks form. Dribble in warm gelatin mixture and continue beating until mixture is stiff. Fold in lemon peel and almonds.

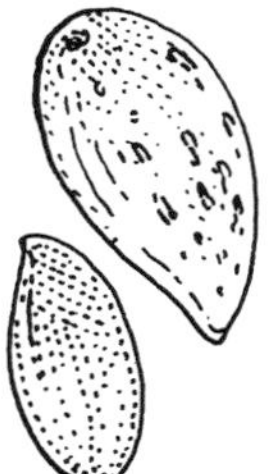

3 Divide mixture evenly into 3 bowls and tint one pink and one green, leaving the third untouched. Lightly grease or spray an 8-cup (2-L) mold and spoon in the pink mixture. Carefully add a layer of white mixture and top with a green layer. Chill for 6 hours.

4 Make custard sauce by combining egg yolks, sugar, salt, lemon peel and milk. Cook, stirring over low heat until the mixture is thick and coats a spoon. Cool.

5 Whip cream and vanilla and gently fold into cooled custard sauce. Store, covered, in refrigerator. Note: Do not whip cream too far in advance of dinner.

Last minute preparation Unmold dessert onto a serving plate. At the table, spoon into individual dishes and top with custard sauce. The colours of this cool and refreshing dessert represent the Mexican flag.

TIME AND TEMPERATURE CHART

8:00	350°F (180°C)	Chicken Mole
8:20	350°F (180°C)	Spanish Rice
8:40	350°F (180°C)	Tacos with Sour Cream
		Green Peas
8:45	350°F (180°C)	Corn with Cream

Scandinavian Menu

First Course	Herring Salad Swedish Meatballs in Mushroom Sauce
Main Course	Fisherman's Loaf with Shrimp Sauce Baked Ham with Spiced Prunes Sweet and Sour Cabbage Potatoes with Anchovies Cucumber and Grape Salad
Dessert	Lemon Delight and Cinnamon Crisps

Co-op Chart

Host/Hostess	Fisherman's Loaf with Shrimp Sauce Baked Ham with Spiced Prunes
Couple A	Swedish Meatballs, Potatoes
Couple B	Herring Salad, Sweet and Sour Cabbage
Couple C	Cucumber and Grape Salad, Lemon Delight and Cinnamon Crisps

Note Since this is a large menu, the quantities for the main dishes have been reduced.

HERRING SALAD

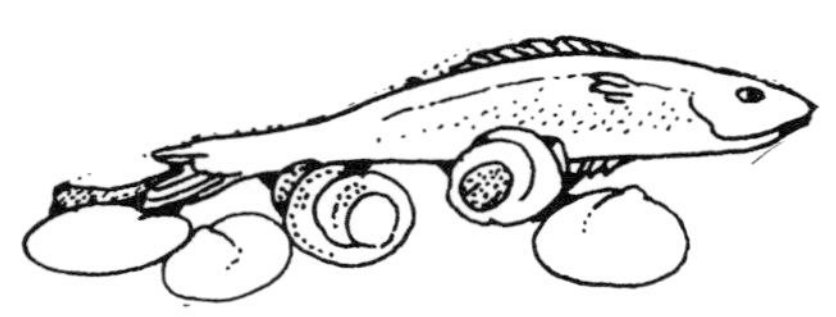

Marinated herring	20 fillets
Onion	3 Tbsp (50 mL) finely chopped
Apple	3 Tbsp (50 mL) finely chopped
Paprika	1/2 tsp (2 mL)
Sour cream	6 Tbsp (100 mL)
Salt	1 tsp (5 mL)
Pepper	1/2 tsp (2 mL)
Lemon	1, sliced
Fresh parsley	6 to 8 sprigs

1 Drain herring and cut into 1-inch (2.5-cm) pieces. Cover and store.

2 Combine onion, apple, paprika, sour cream, salt and pepper. Cover and store in refrigerator.

Last minute preparation Combine dressing and herring and garnish with lemon slices and parsley sprigs.

SWEDISH MEATBALLS IN MUSHROOM SAUCE

Milk	1/2 cup (125 mL)
Dry bread crumbs	1/2 cup (125 mL)
Lean ground beef	1/3 lb (175 g)
Ground pork	1/3 lb (175 g)
Salt	1 1/2 tsp (7 mL)
Pepper	1/8 tsp (0.5 mL)
Fresh parsley	1 tsp (5 mL) chopped
Garlic	1 small clove, minced
Ground nutmeg	1/8 tsp (0.5 mL)
Ground cardamon	1/8 tsp (0.5 mL)
Flour	1/2 cup (125 mL)
Beef stock	2 cups (500 mL)
Butter	1/4 cup (50 mL)
Fresh mushrooms	1/3 cup (75 mL) sliced

1 In a medium-sized bowl combine milk and bread crumbs. Add beef and pork, salt, pepper, parsley, garlic, nutmeg and cardamon and mix well. Refrigerate for 1/2 hour.

2 Roll into 1-inch (2.5-cm) balls and dredge in flour. Reserve flour.

3 Bring stock to a boil and poach meatballs for about 5 minutes, or until they float to surface. Remove meatballs and reserve stock.

4 In a medium-sized frying pan melt 2 Tbsp (25 mL) butter and sauté mushrooms. Remove and set aside.

5 Melt remaining butter in frying pan and add flour used to dredge meatballs. Mix until smooth over medium-high heat. Add reserved stock, stirring constantly.

6 Add meatballs and mushrooms and simmer for 5 minutes. Cool and store, covered, in refrigerator.

Last minute preparation Heat sauce and meatballs over medium heat. Serve steaming hot.

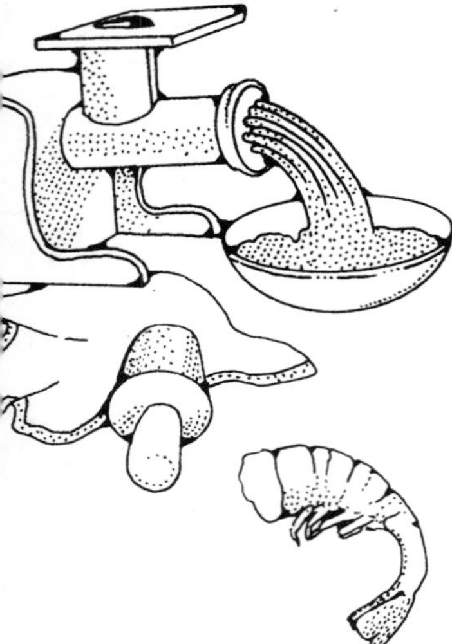

FISHERMAN'S LOAF WITH SHRIMP SAUCE

Haddock or mild white fish	1 1/2 lbs (750 g)
Lemon rind	1 tsp (5 mL)
Salt	2 tsp (10 mL)
Cornstarch	2 Tbsp (30 mL)
Ground nutmeg	1/8 tsp (0.5 mL)
Light cream	1 cup (250 mL)
Milk	3/4 cup (175 mL)
Sauce	
Butter	3 Tbsp (50 mL)
Shelled raw shrimp or lobster	1/2 lb (250 g), coarsely chopped
Green onions	1 Tbsp (15 mL)
White wine	1/2 cup (125 mL)
Flour	7 tsp (35 mL)
Light cream	1 cup (250 mL)
Fresh dill	1 1/2 tsp (7 mL) chopped
Salt	1/4 tsp (1 mL)
Ground nutmeg	1/8 tsp (0.5 mL)

1 Rinse and drain fillets, and cut into small pieces, removing any bones. Sprinkle with lemon rind, salt, cornstarch and nutmeg and purée in blender or food processor, gradually adding light cream and milk.

2 Spoon mixture into a buttered 1-quart (1-L) baking dish. Cover tightly with foil and refrigerate.

3 To make sauce, melt half the butter in a medium-sized saucepan, then add shrimp, green onions and wine and cook for 5 minutes.

4 In another pan, melt rest of butter and add flour, then gradually add cream. Stir constantly until thick and smooth. Remove from heat.

5 Add dill, salt and nutmeg to sauce and combine with shrimp mixture. Cool, cover and refrigerate.

Last minute preparation Partially fill a baking pan with hot water and into it place covered loaf pan containing fish. Bake at 350°F (180°C) for 30 to 35 minutes. Just before fish is ready, gently reheat shrimp sauce. Do not let it boil. When fish loaf is done, invert onto a warmed platter and pour shrimp sauce over top.

BAKED HAM WITH SPICED PRUNES

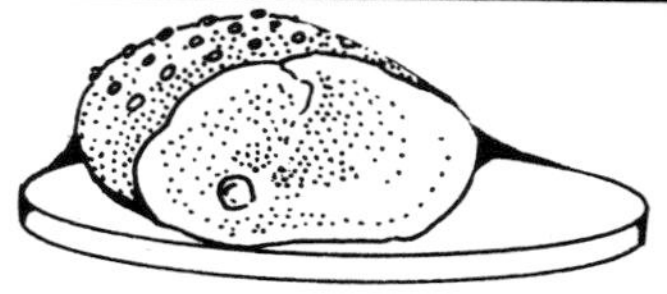

Pitted prunes	1 lb (500 g)
Sugar	1/2 cup (125 mL)
Whole cloves	6
Lemon peel	1 tsp (5 mL) grated
Water	1 1/2 cups (375 mL)
Cooked ham	3 lbs (1 1/2 kg)

1 In a medium-sized saucepan combine prunes, sugar, cloves, lemon peel and water and slowly bring to a boil. Cover and simmer for 20 minutes, then cool.

2 Bake ham at 350°F (180°C) for 1 1/2 hours.

Last minute preparation Reheat prunes in their liquid, then drain. Slice ham and arrange prunes around it.

SWEET AND SOUR CABBAGE

Red cabbage	1 medium head, 3 lbs (1.5 kg)
Butter	1/4 cup (50 mL)
Onion	1 cup (250 mL) chopped
Cider vinegar	1/4 cup (50 mL)
Brown sugar	1/4 cup (50 mL)
Water	1/2 cup (125 mL)
Apples	2 large
Red currant jelly	1/2 cup (125 mL)
Salt	1/2 tsp (2 mL)
Pepper	1/4 tsp (1 mL)

Note Prepare this dish at least 24 hours in advance.

1 Discard tough outer leaves and core and slice cabbage finely.

2 In a heavy saucepan or skillet heat butter and lightly sauté onion. Add cabbage and cook for 5 minutes. Add vinegar, sugar and water and simmer, covered, for about 2 hours or until very tender, or bake at 325°F (160°C) for the same time. Add water during cooking if necessary.

3 Peel, core and grate apples. Remove cabbage from heat and stir in apple, jelly, salt and pepper. Cool, cover and refrigerate.

Last minute preparation Reheat, covered, at 350°F (180°C) until warm throughout, about 25 minutes. Stir occasionally.

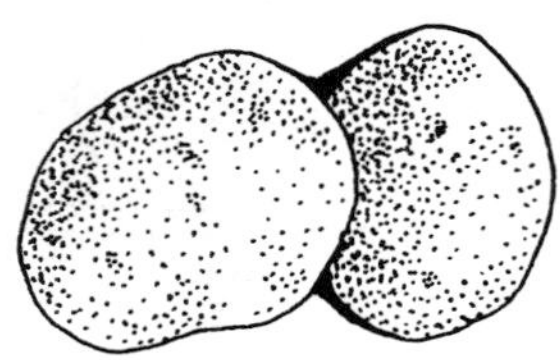

POTATOES WITH ANCHOVIES

Potatoes	8 medium, peeled and sliced
Onions	2 medium, thinly sliced
Anchovy fillets	2 2-oz (50-g) cans, drained
Pepper	1/2 tsp (2 mL)
Sour cream	1 cup (250 mL)
Light cream	1 cup (250 mL)
Butter	2 Tbsp (25 mL)

1 Butter a 2-quart (2-L) casserole. Alternate layers of potato, onion, anchovy and a sprinkling of pepper, ending with potatoes.

2 Heat sour cream and light cream to simmering and add to casserole. Dot with butter, then bake at 350°F (180°C) for one hour. Cool and refrigerate.

Last minute preparation Bake, uncovered, at 350°F (180°C) for 20 minutes. Cover with foil if top is getting too dark.

CUCUMBER AND GRAPE SALAD

Seedless cucumbers	2 medium
Salt	2 tsp (10 mL)
Seedless grapes	3/4 lb (375 g)
Dill seed	3 tsp (15 mL)
Fresh dill leaves	2 tsp (10 mL), if available
Sour cream	1 1/2 cups (375 mL)
Tabasco sauce	dash
Pepper	1/2 tsp (2 mL)
Paprika	1 tsp (5 mL)

1 Thinly slice unpeeled cucumbers. Sprinkle with salt and drain in colander for 30 minutes. Rinse under cold water and drain again. Combine with washed grapes.

2 Combine dill seed and leaves, sour cream, Tabasco, pepper and paprika. Cover and chill.

Last minute preparation Combine dressing with grapes and cucumber and toss well. Serve cold.

LEMON DELIGHT

Unflavoured gelatin	1 envelope
Fresh lemon juice	6 Tbsp (100 mL)
Eggs	5, separated
Sugar	3/4 cup (175 mL)
Lemon rind	1 Tbsp (15 mL)
Whipping cream	1 cup (250 mL)

1 In a small saucepan add gelatin to lemon juice and heat gently until dissolved. Cool.

2 Beat egg yolks with sugar until almost white, about 5 minutes. Add gelatin and grated lemon rind and mix well.

3 Beat egg whites until stiff but not dry, then fold into lemon mixture.

4 Beat whipping cream until stiff, then gently fold into lemon mixture. Spoon into serving bowl or individual dishes. Cover and refrigerate.

Last minute preparation Serve cold with cinnamon crisps.

CINNAMON CRISPS

Butter	1 cup (250 mL)
Sugar	1 1/2 cups (375 mL)
Eggs	2
Vanilla extract	1 tsp (5 mL)
All-purpose flour	1 3/4 cups (450 mL) sifted
Baking powder	2 tsp (10 mL)
Cinnamon	3 Tbsp (50 mL)
Walnut pieces	1/2 cup (125 mL) finely chopped
Sugar	2 Tbsp (25 mL)

1 Cream butter and gradually add sugar. Beat in eggs and vanilla.

2 Sift flour, baking powder and 1 Tbsp (15 mL) cinnamon. Add to creamed mixture and blend well. Chill for 30 minutes.

3 Combine walnuts with remaining 2 Tbsp (25 mL) cinnamon and 2 Tbsp (25 mL) sugar.

4 Roll chilled dough into walnut-sized balls, then roll in walnut mixture. Place on a greased cookie sheet, about 2 inches (5 cm) apart. Bake at 400°F (200°C) until lightly golden, about 8 to 10 minutes.

TIME AND TEMPERATURE CHART

7:30	350°F (180°C)	Baked Ham
8:10	Stove top	Meatballs
8:25	350°F (180°C)	Fisherman's Loaf
8:35	350°F (180°C)	Sweet and Sour Cabbage
8:40	350°F (180°C)	Potatoes with Anchovies

Index